CHEMISTRY ON THE COURT:
The Untold Story of a #1 Team

By Mel Eaton Matuszak

2005

PURE HEART PRESS
MAIN STREET RAG PUBLISHING COMPANY
CHARLOTTE, NORTH CAROLINA

Copyright © 2005 Mel Eaton Matuszak

Acknowledgements:

Some of the photos that were used came from the 1958 and 1959 Kansas State University Yearbooks.

Photograph page 14 courtesy of the *K-Stater Magazine*

Library of Congress Control Number: 2005906153

ISBN 1-930907-86-9

Produced in the United States of America

Pure Heart Press/
Main Street Rag Publishing Company
4416 Shea Lane
Charlotte. NC 28227
www.MainStreetRag.com

KANSAS STATE vs MISSOURI U.

Table of Contents

A Tribute	1
A Completely Different Time	3
1957-58: Seeking the Magic Mix	23
1958-59: A Patched-Together Team	67
Recap of the Games	115
Forty Years Later	151
Afterword	159

This book is dedicated to all of the people I've met through Kansas State University who are now a part of my soul and character, and especially to the members of those teams who inspired this book.

A TRIBUTE

Fred "Tex" Winter stands today as one of basketball's greatest living legends, having actively coached for an amazing 58 years (as of the 2005-06 season), more than any other coach in the game's history. Even more amazing is the influence he's had on those whose lives he's touched. His players, to a man, respect him and speak highly of his impact on their playing and non-playing years. He taught them not only the game of basketball, but also the game of life and how to play it fairly. It's not been uncommon for players to send their sons to play under Tex Winter, no matter where he happened to be coaching.

Fond and amusing memories are constantly relived by many of his players, and Tex never tires of hearing them or bringing up some of his own. One of his quirks was his fumbling of names, particularly of the opponents. As one player mused at a tribute dinner for Tex, "He always called you by name. It may not have been yours, however!"

The former players share jokes at his expense, speaking perhaps of his legendary brown suit that he wore continuously through many games because he considered it "lucky." The players say that suit could walk to the game by itself. Tex's choice of fashion-defying ties precipitated a barrage of outrageous ties as a gift by one team. They thought it hilarious, but Tex seemed appreciative.

The players' respect for Tex Winter has never wavered. He tolerated no foul language, no bad sportsmanship, and no lackadaisical play. He expected good grades, good manners, and good effort. No player was exempt from these standards.

Besides Tex Winter's outstanding record as a coach, his contributions to the game overall have been significant. He, along with his Kansan friend Ken Mahoney, invented some devices that helped teach or refine the game. These include the toss back, the snap-back rims that permitted the "dunk," and the short skirt backboard. His book on the Triangle Offense is in its third printing and has been published in several foreign languages. It is considered one of the best books on the strategy of the game. Coaches on all levels have attended his seminars and viewed his videos, and come to him for advice and mentoring. His influence on the game and its future has been immeasurable.

Tex should have a Hall of Fame of his own. He could fill it with letters, testimonials, inventions, and all of his works and speeches. His honors have included Coach of the Year, President of the National Association of Basketball Coaches, recipient of 9 NBA rings, the prestigious John Bunn Award from the Basketball Hall of Fame, the Naismith Award for outstanding contributions, and more – yet those who have known him recall his humility and honesty. He is the personification of good character, and that legacy is perhaps his most important to basketball history.

This story is an account of two of his very early years of coaching: 1957-58 and 1958-59, years that he describes as defining years when he established himself among the top college coaches in the country. He believed those two teams were the best college teams he coached and the most interesting.

A COMPLETELY DIFFERENT TIME

We closed the door on the condo and, in our minds, on the outside world. We had come to Hilton Head Island for a respite to re-charge our spirit and get away from the constant details – the details of setting up a new business, frequent trips all over the country, and the phone ringing, ringing, ringing…

It *was* ringing! I hurried to set my suitcase down and grabbed the phone. My husband came to stand by my side. He knew that only our daughters had this number – just in case. My voice shook slightly as I answered. The voice on the other end was frantic, "*MomIknowyousaidnottobotheryoubutthisisreallyanemergency!*" It was our younger daughter, Joelyn, calling from California. My throat was dry and barely able to utter the question, "What's wrong? Slow down and tell me what's happened."

She managed to talk while sobbing out a story about a wild kitten that was sick and needed a vet…and, she might need some money. We, of course, agreed to help. She had already found a good vet. "And he knows Dad! He remembers him very well!" She had noticed that the veterinarian's degree was from Kansas State and said to him that her folks had gone there. When he asked our names and she said "Matuszak," he exclaimed, "Not *Don* Matuszak?!"

As a teenager, the vet had listened on the radio to the Kansas State basketball games and definitely knew the name Matuszak.

He told our daughter how great that team had been, and that he chose Kansas State partly because of that team.

How many times had we heard similar remembrances – for 40 plus years! So many people remember that team and those years. We have moved many times during our marriage and frequently have run into someone who remembers the name Matuszak and those games.

Soon after our college graduation, it was no surprise to hear someone question Don about a certain game, a particular play, or one of his teammates. I especially remember giving birth to our first daughter, Jill, and the obstetrician and Don sitting at my bedside while I was in labor. They were deep into a discussion about a particular game and the doctor was interested in a certain strategy. As I felt the pains coming more frequently I'd say, "Doctor…I think it's happening," and he would kindly nod toward me and reassuringly say, "It'll be a while; this is not a quick process," as he continued the conversation. I barely made it into the operating room in time!

Twenty years later while living in Salt Lake City, a neurosurgeon looked at my last name and asked, "Any relation to the Don Matuszak who used to play basketball?" When I told him it was one and the same, he told me he'd been in a Matuszak fan club when he was in high school in Norman, Oklahoma, and that admittance to the club hinged on being able to do things like passing the ball over your back to a teammate while running forward, or dribbling the ball around your legs and behind your back. (No, my bill from the neurosurgeon wasn't any less, but it seemed easier to pay.)

Skip to this past year when I found a flyer in our mailbox. The man who left the flyer had just moved to our area from Michigan and was skilled in laying carpet. Just the service I needed, so I called him. He was very nice and we chatted while he worked. I mentioned that his state had some great football teams and that we also had one at Kansas State. "Oh, but your school had some great basketball teams back in the late '50s, I think it was," he said. "I am really a basketball fan."

The stories go on and my wellspring keeps bubbling. Yearly trips to our alma mater and various alumni events continue to feed me. "I remember that one game where…" someone says, or, "It was a special time to be in college, particularly at K-State," or "What happened to us in the finals?"

The names, the times, the era, the coaches of the late '50s teams keep cropping up. Our phone still rings occasionally and an old friend wants to chat with Don about the old days, or a sports writer wants to question him about those teams or requests a comment on his former coach, Tex Winter.

The details of those two teams have often been glossed over or mixed up, but nearly everyone remembers that Coach Tex Winter launched his successful career in those years. They also remember that there was a #1 team at Kansas State, sometime, somehow.

This book was precipitated by several things: never-ending questions from people who are sincerely interested in knowing about "that #1 team," and the partial or incorrect reporting in other stories and books about that team. Coach Tex Winter once admitted that his memory sometimes confuses the two teams he coached back in 1957-58 and 1958-59. Many alumni and sports aficionados confuse them too.

When I began to gather this information I first went to the players, themselves, for their recollections. Then I turned to every available source: old newspapers, old sports magazines, lists from the National Basketball Hall of Fame, lists from the Big 12 office, and NCAA records. I searched microfiche files at libraries. My intent was to be as factual as possible and I believe I've achieved my goal.

This is the story that has never been told. It's about that #1 team – a team that defied all logic, all odds, yet whose picture has never even been displayed in the school's basketball arena.

***

Over the years I've watched the exciting and challenging game of basketball evolve into something I no longer recognize as the sport we loved in the 1950s. Athletes of past generations played for the thrill of the sport and love of the game, not for future fame or money. If a player happened to be good enough he might go on to play professionally, but the money was not the motivator, for salaries then were a pittance compared to today's payouts.

Before we can relive the story of those teams, we must picture that generation and the attitudes and values of that period. In recreating the picture, I've included many details that are personal – about student life and the behavioral norms that were common then.

The times and the social scene were completely different than they are now. Compared to today, it was a time of innocence. Our lives were much simpler, and our world much more restrictive, particularly in small town Kansas, where I grew up. People generally did not travel the distances we do today. There were no interstate highways and airfare was expensive. There were few motels along the roads, anyway, so it was not a particularly easy or cheap task to drive a long distance.

The usual form of communication was a letter. On the envelope we affixed a three-cent stamp. Long distance phone calls were expensive, used for emergencies or very important news. We didn't miss what we didn't have, though, and there was a great spirit of community in our small towns.

As I travel in memory back to the '50s, I peel away years of cultural changes, to an era before computers, cell phones, DVDs, color television, and even (gasp) ballpoint pens! There couldn't have been a more ideal time to be in college, particularly in Kansas – the heart of the heartland, one of the friendliest places on earth – where everyone spoke to everyone else, whether stranger or old friend. Farmers drove with one hand on the wheel, the other one propped up ready to wave. Our values were rooted in the everyday business of making a living, a rather simple living, with an eye toward helping a neighbor, a friend, or family member.

My small town of Harper, Kansas, was about 60 miles from the city of Wichita and I had no idea how far it was from Kansas City because that was beyond my range of thinking. My world was quite contained and fulfilled right there in that small friendly farming community. Our small town was typical of many in Kansas. It served the farmers and their families and offered its residents a sense of togetherness and belonging. Most everyone in town was acquainted and many of the families had lived in the area for generations. "You know so-and-so's daughter? She's going to move to Texas." And, "Did you hear that the such-and-such family was hit hard by the tornado? But their neighbors all helped harvest their crop this year."

We were between wars. The Korean War had come to a close, and we had no way of knowing that the conflict in Vietnam was on the horizon. Life on the home front was comfortable. We were gradually recovering from the effects of World War II and getting back on our feet as a nation. Some young men of our community had lost their lives in that war. The ones who returned showed a maturity that earned our respect and awe. The veterans brought back tales of foreign places and distant cities, but generally kept the battlefield details to themselves.

Quite abruptly a new invention came on the market. It was called television and appeared in the guise of a little box – a box with a 10- or 12-inch screen displaying a snowy picture that often had a horizontal bar rolling across it. Usually there were three channels available when you turned the dial. The fuzzy images were in black and white (or shades of gray) – but we could see live shows! People in Hollywood and other places were now in front of us on this little screen, and we could see and hear them as they performed! The comedians we had heard on the radio – Jack Benny, George Burns and Gracie Allen, Uncle Miltie, and Lucille Ball – were right there, *in our own houses* talking and making us laugh. We saw our cowboy heroes, Gene Autry and Roy Rogers, in Western shows. We could tune in to American Bandstand with host Dick Clark and catch up on the fashions of other teenagers – the bobby sox crowd – and learn the latest dance steps and hear popular singers such as Pat Boone, Frankie Avalon, and Bobby Darin. Places we had only heard about were now a visual reality: New York, California, and Chicago.

    The new phenomenon of television ever so gently swept us toward a new way of life and broke open our cocoon of predictability. Its effects were subtle, slowly seeping into our culture, invading our lives, and reshaping our thinking and our world. Our small corner of the world suddenly became an inclusive part of the world. We danced the same dances they danced in Chicago; we imitated fashions we saw teens in other places wearing; we envisioned dreams we could not have imagined before television. The doors to our insular world had been thrown wide open!

    Television programming ran in the afternoons and evenings. People began planning their calendars to include time for gathering and watching their favorite shows. Even if your family didn't have a TV, as was the case with my family, you heard from others what was going on with this new contraption – a contraption referred to by some as an "idiot box." Watching television became a social event. We assembled in a circle around the small screen, trying to get a good view. Some people added magnifiers: large sheets taped to the screen. With this addition you had to get a straight-ahead view or you'd see a distorted picture. Others imaginatively added "color" to the screen by taping on cellophane paper with strips in different colors. Those first television sets were expensive – around $400. A new car sold for about $2,000 then, and tuition for a year in college was around $150, so few families could afford the luxury of television. Sooner or later, though, we all gathered to witness this miracle of technology, and news of what was going on in television land was often the focus of our conversation.

Even though my family did not have a television, some neighboring families did. It seemed, however, that the sets were broken most of the time, and few people were schooled in television repair. There were other interests, though – such as "dragging Main" to show off cars and see who was in town; piling in a car and going to dances in nearby towns; and seeing movies at drive-in theaters. Also, of course, every town regardless of size offered lots of sports activities.

Although traditional by nature, we down-to-earth folks of the Midwest could see that our world was changing in diverse ways. The predictability of our lives was threatened. The older generations, who were used to seeing family farms passed to younger generations, watched as their youngsters came under the influence of rock and roll, Bermuda shorts, poodle skirts, crew cuts, and strange lingo. A young new singer named Elvis was raising eyebrows with his gyrating dancing and sexy look. He shocked the older generations but fascinated the younger ones.

The seasoned generations saw change coming quickly and realized the change was inevitable. The young were eager and restless to be a part of the newness – wanted to scoop up this new and exciting life in big shovelfuls.

Many of us realized that education was the key to opening doors of opportunity.

It never entered my mind that there was an option *other* than college. My mom had enjoyed a rather privileged upbringing and went away for two years to the university. She always talked about "when you go to college." She was one of the rare single parents of that era, yet she never spoke of the financial strain a college education would be – she expected my high school years to be followed by college years. Mom said college would give me better choices, and help me develop a wider circle of friends and come to maturity within a good setting. She had attended Kansas University, but she let me make my own decision about which school to attend.

A local boy whom I'd always admired attended Kansas State College (as it was then known) and he dropped by one weekend when he was home and brought along a fraternity brother who was visiting. They spoke highly of their school and urged me to apply. Both conveyed their strong feelings about the academics of the school, the friendly people, and asked me about my interests. They asked which program I would be studying. I said perhaps Home Economics or English, maybe even veterinary medicine. Their reaction was the same to all my answers: K-State was just the place!

That was how my college decision was made – right then and there. If it was good enough for these two good-looking, personable and quite able young men, then that was where I wanted to go. I had no idea what I'd study, where the school was, or what the campus looked like. I do remember hearing that it was an "agricultural college," but I knew people could study other subjects there as well. We had no money for frivolous things like visiting the campus before enrolling, and absolutely no knowledge about applying for a possible scholarship. At play, perhaps, was the nagging reality that if we asked for information we'd have to divulge that I had a father who contributed nothing to our income. Nevertheless, I made plans to attend Kansas State.

Manhattan, Kansas. It seemed far away, a long three-hour drive. I began to think of being on my own for the first time, of leaving my small town in the southern part of the state. The switch to college would entail major upheaval and a big adjustment, but I was mentally ready. My high school had, at most, thirty people in the graduating class, and the students had been cliquish. I had never felt like I belonged in any of the groups. I was one of the few who had no father around, quite an unusual situation in those times. My father was an alcoholic, something we couldn't and didn't talk about. We didn't lie about it; my mother was adamant about telling the truth. She cautioned us, "You are no better than your word." We usually said Dad was working out of the state, which in fact he was, though we never knew where.

In the summers we always went to Oklahoma to visit my father's family, at least a four-hour drive. That was the farthest I had ever been from home. The trip was considered a big undertaking and a boring one at that. We took the bus, and my brother and I usually got to sit up front by the driver where we could enjoy an unobstructed view. My mother hovered close by and made up games to keep us busy. We counted turtles, dead and alive, in the road. We followed all the billboards, trying to locate each succeeding letter of the alphabet. And we eagerly read the Burma Shave signs. Sometimes we'd write down some of the jingles so we could tell our aunts and uncles in Oklahoma about the funniest ones. The Burma Shave advertisement consisted of five signs in a row. Once your attention was captured, you watched for the next sign and then the next, to get the rhyming safety message: " Don't lose your head…To gain a minute…You need your head…Your brains are in it…*Burma Shave.*" Another good one: "Passing school zone…Take it slow…Let our little…Shavers grow…*Burma Shave*." This pastime kept us from asking the driver quite so often, "How much longer?"

When the day came at last for the long trip to Kansas State – my school! – my emotions reeled. My mother and grandmother loaded my grandmother's car with my large suitcase and a box or two of belongings as we prepared for the trip to Manhattan, Kansas. I had carefully packed the requisite clothes that I knew would be in fashion: several circular skirts, and some straight ones; a crinoline petticoat (it had to be secured with rubber bands to get it to fit inside the trunk); sweaters and blouses; saddle oxfords and loafers, and bobby sox; several dressy dresses, plus high heels and gloves (for teas and dressy events); and intimate apparel, including a new girdle.

Mom had made sandwiches so we could stop for lunch at a roadside park in Wichita, about 60 miles away. I still distinctly remember that I had no appetite; my stomach was not interested in food. We then continued our drive for several more hours over the small blacktop highways to our destination and followed the directions to my designated dormitory. I had been assigned a room and a roommate, and held tightly to the instructions telling me where I was supposed to go and when. As soon as Mom helped me inside and looked around to her satisfaction, she decided it was time for her to leave and let me adjust on my own. She and my grandmother had decided to make this excursion a grand vacation, so they were continuing on to visit a friend in Kansas City; they needed to be on their way while there was still daylight. My mom left me with only this bit of sage wisdom: "You will be a little fish in a big pond, but you'll remember these years by the friends you make."

She was right in both respects. Although lost, confused, and anxious, I began to make new friends within a few weeks. I found others who were walking in the same alien zone with the same emotional quandary. Many of them were also on the campus and in Manhattan for the first time. Everyone was friendly, though, and whenever there was eye contact we followed it with a greeting. Professors went out of their way to make the new freshmen feel at home. Since most classes were small we had the opportunity to get acquainted with the others in the class and with the professors. Girls in the dorm were friendly too, and we had lots of room get-togethers and hall parties. I felt like I was acquiring a new and larger family – a family that accepted me immediately.

The school sponsored get-acquainted dances on the tennis courts, and other "mixers." The dorms planned dances, and social hours or teas, all designed to welcome the freshmen. I experienced the warmth of belonging and found that adjusting to college was much easier than I had feared.

There were about 6,800 students at the school then. The charm of the campus appealed to me: small curving pathways, old buildings of native limestone that seemed to fit naturally next to more modern ones. I loved walking around discovering something new each day: new niches, unusual plantings, different buildings, new people, and always a distinct scent of the season in the air. Soon, familiarity made me comfortable and secure.

At the beginning I got lost and kept referring to my map, always careful to listen to the bells that signaled a change of class. The bells were located in Anderson Hall, K-State's oldest and most prominent building. It housed the administration offices and has always been the hallmark of Kansas State. I passed by it frequently during the day on my way to classes, often using it as a landmark to locate the building I was seeking. Anderson was my favorite building because its Romanesque design fascinated me. I'd never seen similar architecture on anything other than a church. The building reminded me of my distant dream to spread my wings and visit faraway lands, see places I'd only read or heard about, and surround myself with other cultures.

Kansas State students were sometimes referred to (especially by students at Kansas University) as "Aggies," derived from the school's previous name, Kansas State Agricultural College. Our school had the distinction of being the first land grant college named by the Morrill Land Grant Act of 1862. The land act helped establish schools which would emphasize agricultural and mechanical arts, while also offering scientific and classical studies. In Kansas, the wheat capital of the United States, such a school was an appropriate beginning. Kansas State is located about 125 miles west and slightly north of Kansas City, and 50 miles from the state capitol in Topeka. It sits at the junction of the Big Blue and Kansas Rivers near the town of Manhattan. The town is approximately four miles from the campus. Back in the '50s the town had two hospitals, several department stores, shoe stores, a theater, specialty clothing shops, cafes, restaurants, and several bars and clubs on the outskirts of the town. The population was approximately 22,000 in 1958, and that number included the students living on campus. Manhattan often was and still is referred to as the "Little Apple."

Immediately adjacent to the campus is a small community known as Aggieville, within easy walking

Aggieville in the 1950s

distance. That detail was important in the '50s because very few students had cars. There were bookstores, a drug store, a theater, shoe repair shop, several clothing places, and hamburger joints and bars that were popular student hangouts.

Just as Mom had predicted I made lots of new friends. Also, I somehow figured out that you didn't always have to attend class; you could get by if you just passed the tests. It certainly sounded easy and, since I had excelled in my small high school, I proceeded to operate on that assumption, until the dreaded semester finals. My many activities had taken a toll on my academics and I was operating on shaky ground. Phoning long-distance was rare and expensive, but I called Mom. She remained positive as she recounted to me the main thing she had gotten from her college years: a great social life and good friends; but I knew that times were different now than in Mom's day and I really needed an education. Besides, the cost of my education was putting a strain on the family's finances, and here I was, certainly not making the most of the opportunity.

Finally a moment of realization told me I needed to make some money and also to gain more maturity. I was only 17 when I entered college; I needed to grow up and get more serious about my future. A new friend in my dorm felt the same way, so we made up our minds to take a year off from school. This was a major decision. Usually this route signaled that you were a dropout or quitter. Once you enrolled in college you were expected to stay four years and get a degree. My family was naturally disappointed, but they supported me in my effort.

My girlfriend and I both found good jobs and took an apartment in Wichita, and spent that summer and the next school year working, saving money, and gaining maturity and independence. We had promised each other we'd return the next year – no matter what. And I did enroll as a sophomore. She married my brother who had returned from the Navy, and they began their married life in Manhattan. He started school and she began a new job. It was an ideal arrangement for me, to have them close by.

When I returned to Manhattan the place seemed like a familiar friend. That first week was filled with moving, unpacking, setting up appointments with advisors, enrolling in classes – plus the excitement of greeting old friends and meeting new ones. Classes began right after Labor Day and it wasn't long before the summer heat turned to crisp and glorious days of autumn. Everyone settled in for the 1956-57 school year.

The focal point of the landscape was the brand new Student Union, a beautiful three-story building that catered to a student's every need. It quickly became the social mecca for the student body. At the time it was deemed one of the top five campus unions in the country, a reputation that was well deserved. From the parking lot or lower level the doors opened to a small dance floor with four or five small, intimate tables and a juke box which, at three songs for a quarter, thumped out Elvis Presley's "You Ain't Nothin' but a Hound Dog," or Bobby Darin's hopping vocals on "Splish, Splash, I Was Taking a Bath!" Or you could pick out a slow-dance favorite by Dean Martin, the McGuire Sisters, Johnny Mathis; or a raspy favorite of mine, Fats Domino's "Blueberry Hill." Students liked to use this spot for one-on-one conversation, or to just relax or study, with their special music in the background. Perhaps because it was too open to the daylight and the public, no dancing ever seemed to take place. Right next door was the bowling alley, where students could practice their bowling skills when the facility wasn't being used for recreation courses. If you proceeded up the stairs or walked in from street level to the main student lounge, the scene was entirely different. Students were everywhere – at small and large tables, roaming the halls, snacking or eating a meal. Some were on dates.

The Union was a great setting for the inexpensive dates we called "Coke dates." The guys were expected to pay the bill for any kind of date, so sipping soft drinks in a neutral space made sense. Both brief and cheap, the Coke dates were preferred by almost everyone as get-acquainted first dates.

The air in the Union was rich with the heavy scent of homemade cinnamon rolls and coffee, while clouds of cigarette smoke hovered and mingled overhead. Yes, quite a few students smoked, and it was considered the acceptable thing to do. Ads on TV and radio and in magazines touted the glamorous look of holding your cigarette while conversing with your friends.

Students mixed freely in this big one-room gathering place on the main floor. You could order food or drink from early morning to late night. The tables and chairs seemed always to be filled with people chattering at the highest threshold the human ear could stand. Everyone mingled. Our Kansan upbringing was evident as we made sure all were greeted: international students, fraternity boys, sorority girls, dorm residents, athletes, professors, blacks, whites, males, and females.

Sometimes I met with study groups from a class, to work on a project or just to visit. Other times I talked with some of the international students, interpreting some of our American slang – like the word of the day, "cool," which we dragged out for emphasis. I tried to help them develop an ear for the nuances of English. Professors occasionally announced that they would be in the Union at a designated time – to help students who needed extra help.

At the beginning of the year I had widened my circle of friends by joining a sorority. This gave me endless opportunities for adapting, learning about life skills, and for putting the needed emphasis on my studies. The sorority required attention to all facets of life, particularly making good grades. It helped me straighten out my priorities and establish new study habits. I became a student, finally!

Social life was busy, too, particularly for the female population, as they enjoyed a lop-sided ratio of 2 ½ males to each female! With all the events sponsored by the living groups and the school, it was unusual to spot a stranger on campus. Curfews set at 11:00 p.m. on weeknights and 1:00 a.m. on weekends were actively enforced and probably helped keep things in balance. There was also the morality code of the times that we never thought to question. We were not to be "damaged goods," as my mother bluntly put it, or "second hand property."

My grandmother added, "Virtue never goes out of style." She often told me this.

As I've worked on this book, the rediscovery of the morality of those times has given my memory a jolt. Why, we didn't even say the word "sex," and certainly did not say the more intimate terms used freely today. We were careful about every touch of the hand, every body movement – for we didn't want any move to be misinterpreted. Never on television or in movies did we see a couple in bed together. There was restraint evident in the way women were treated, even a reverence toward women. Talking back to a parent was almost unheard-of, and teachers warranted special respect.

Clothing, too, was conservative. No dress code existed on campus, but girls wore long skirts and sweaters or blouses to class, with the usual saddles or loafers and bobby sox, hiding all but a little of the leg. Even the cheerleaders' attire was much the same. Everyone dressed neatly, though not extravagantly; shirts were tucked in, haircuts short for the guys and usually mid to long for the females. Some girls opted for the stylish ponytails seen on TV. For church, dress night in the living areas on Thursdays, and Sunday teas we donned nice dresses, heels and hose, and sometimes gloves. Evening dresses were either long or mid-length, and nearly always full-skirted. There was not a hint of anything slinky or tight fitting. Surprisingly, however, strapless formal wear was often worn, a fact that now looks incongruous beside the other styles of the day. Sometimes gloves, either short or past the elbow, completed the look. The only times these fashion dictates were lifted was during final week or study week, or events like a picnic or pep rally. Then we could wear jeans. Sneakers had not yet been invented.

Obviously, I can't speak for everyone, but any sexual activity before marriage was a giant no-no. Guys were warned by their parents that if they got a girl in trouble, they either had to marry her or join the Army. A girl was cautioned that becoming pregnant would shame the family, and that the baby would probably have to be given up unless the boy agreed to marry. We girls dressed and acted in accordance with these expectations. We also had a last line of defense: our girdles. Why we wore them I can't explain even now, but we did. I suppose they gave us a sleeker look. With all the walking, very few of us really needed them, but they were the fashion. I weighed 112 pounds at the time, yet faithfully squeezed my small frame into the darned thing nearly every day. Garters attached to the girdle secured our expensive silk stockings. (When pantyhose were finally introduced, we women considered the invention a great historical step forward.)

My upbringing was a bit unusual, to say the least. Not only was there no father around to mold my idea of how a family interacts, but my mother had had a sheltered upbringing and even as open as she tried to be, her naiveté could not shed much light on the facts of life. One particular incident comes to mind. Mom had always told me that if I had questions about anything, she wanted me to come to her and ask them, not to learn the answers in the alley or behind the barn. So, one night I decided to ask. She was waiting up for me, as usual, when I came in from an evening with friends, and I sat on her bed and sought an answer to something I'd just heard. "What," I said, "is a homosexual?" Mom looked bewildered. I continued, "You know – where a man loves a man and a woman loves a woman."

Mom looked puzzled, and pondered this for a long moment before she finally said, "Honey, I don't think they had those when I was growing up."

Asking my older brother was simply out of the question. I could never have talked about such things with him.

As I became more attuned to the campus and the surroundings again, everyone seemed to be talking about the upcoming basketball season. I had enjoyed high school sports, but was not an educated fan. The excitement on campus, though, made it clear to me that the season ahead merited my attention. I joined my fellow students and dressed in the school colors, purple and white. We gave our rousing support to the teams. Willie the Wildcat was our mascot, and a favorite cheer was, "Everyman a Wildcat!" Sometimes the after-chant was, "And all the women, too!" Our football team was not really a contender (were usually at the bottom of the conference), but they provided many fun and exciting Saturday afternoons and we heartily cheered them. It was the basketball season, though, that we eagerly awaited.

On our small campus we knew most of the athletes. They were the guys we sat by in class, talked with in the Union – just regular guys, not the idolized jocks of today. Several of the front tables in the Union accommodated as many as 10-12 people, and the athletes and their friends often occupied these spots. They were all friendly, and greeted students and professors that passed by. Their laughter was contagious as they told jokes and shared stories. The tables weren't strictly for athletes; anybody was welcome.

Many of the athletes lived in West Stadium, the only dorm on campus for men. Guys that didn't live in West Stadium lived in frat houses, or at home (a "townie"), or in an apartment – often someone's basement.

Our basketball team "caught fire" – definitely met our expectations. In my second year they eventually posted a 15-8 season and took second place in the conference race, right behind the KU team who had as their center the nationally renowned Wilt Chamberlain.

One of my sorority sisters was from Ames, Iowa, so we followed the team to the game there in the late part of the season and stayed at her home. At an after-game party, one of our players asked for a ride back to the team's quarters and we let him squeeze in with our group. Within minutes he had us all laughing. I'd never been around anyone quite like him – a tinge of brashness, yet an ease and humor that captivated us all. His rapid-fire dialect included "dese," "dose," and "dem." I was fascinated!

This was not the typical boy meets girl, they fall in love, they date during college, and eventually they marry. First there was a problem even arranging a first date. He called me several weeks after we met. I checked my calendar and said, "Yes, I'd like to go out with you, but it'll have to be in about six weeks." (Remember the ratio?)

He showed little emotion on the phone and offhandedly replied, "Okay, maybe I'll call again another time."

That, of course, perked up my interest. (I still find that difficult to explain.) Somehow, someway, we did eventually have an official Coke date. He borrowed someone's car and picked me up at the dorm. We drove a short distance from campus to a drive-in restaurant where we ordered coffee and just sat and visited. As we finished he said something like, "Jus' t'row de sack out de winda,

Babe." My first thought was that this was how gangsters in movies talked! I moved closer to the handle of the passenger door. But as we continued to get acquainted, he continued to intrigue me, and his humor was refreshing. We ended up having a delightful conversation and he gave me a goodnight kiss as he walked me to the door. (I still had the imprint of the door handle on my side.)

For an upcoming formal dance I needed a date. As I eliminated all the possible invitees, he entered my mind. It was a bold move, but why not?!

We double-dated with another couple. My brother invited us all to his apartment for a before-party drink. Until only a year before that, I had thought having a drink made you an alcoholic, but on this fun evening I joined in the frivolity and sipped on a drink. During the rest of the evening I found myself laughing, somewhat at ease, and trying hard to interpret what my date was saying. I'd never heard a Chicago accent or heard anyone speak with such rapidity. I was delighted to find that he was a good dancer. The drink or two, however, proved too much for me early in the evening. As social chairman of the sorority, I stood in the receiving line and leaned – yes, *leaned* – on the Dean of Students!

The school year was soon over. We said goodbye to our friends. My new "friend" and I said goodbye in the parking lot behind the Union in a crowd of about 200 other people. Our farewell was a quick, "See you next fall."

1957-58: SEEKING THE MAGIC MIX

The first days of school kept us bustling about, enrolling, moving in, settling into our living quarters. A task I dreaded was "pulling cards" for classes, a ritual that required us to make out schedules and "pull" the punch card from the keeper of the cards. When we had assembled the right cards for the right classes we could breathe a big sigh of relief. If, however, a class was full, we had to rearrange our schedule and perhaps go through the process again. That was the data processing system of the time.

Classes began, and before long the football season had come and gone. Our team had put up some admirable fights against tough Big 7 opponents that included Oklahoma and non-conference Michigan State – both ranked #1 in the nation at the time we played them.

On the basketball radar screen, we were considered one of the teams to watch. Our Big Seven Conference – which included Kansas, Iowa State, Nebraska, Colorado, Oklahoma, and Missouri – had been tagged to become the Big Eight, with the addition of Oklahoma State. The conference looked full of good talent, particularly the new sophomores. At Kansas University, Wilt Chamberlain, the 7-foot phenomenon who had played as a sophomore the previous year, was returning with a well-deserved reputation as a mighty force on the court. Chamberlain had taken his team to the Final Four where, in a hard-fought game against North Carolina, they had taken second in the tournament.

Coach "Tex" Winter was now in his fifth season as our head coach. He had finished his first few seasons with mediocre 11-10 records. Some fans, impatient and demanding, had posted signs around campus that read, "Spring is here. Winter must go."

The alumni and town people liked Tex: he was quiet, affable, and very good looking. His dark, thick hair and even features didn't go unnoticed by the female students. Only six feet in height, his solid frame and competitive nature had made him an outstanding athlete in high school and college, where he excelled in pole vaulting and basketball. The people *liked* him; there was nothing to dislike, except his record, which needed to show more wins.

But last year's team had done well. They had finished the season with a 15-8 record, 2nd behind KU in the conference. K-State was considered to have a chance at competing for the title this year. Last year they had added height and skill in their sophomore class: Bob Boozer, a 6'8" forward who had shown signs of greatness in his debut season; Don Matuszak, a 5'11" guard who was a capable ball handler and scrapper; and Jim Holwerda, who had proven that he was a stalwart substitute with a great outside shot. This combo joined older reliables like Roy DeWitz, a hustling and tenacious guard/forward; Jack Parr, a determined and talented rebounder and scorer; Hayden Abbott, known as a hard-nosed competitor; and Larry Fischer and Dean Plagge, steady reserves.

Of the "old veterans," Hayden Abbott was probably the most surprised to have even been offered a scholarship. He suffered from a chronic back problem and had missed playing basketball his senior year in high school, but Howie Shannon, the assistant coach, had seen him play and remembered him and his potential. Tex took Howie's word and offered Hayden a scholarship. Hayden became known for his quick, go-to-the-rim ability.

No one had seen Roy DeWitz play, but Tex had read about him in the news coverage in Illinois. Roy was a small, fiery competitor, the kind Tex wanted to add to his mix. Tex and Howie visited Roy in Illinois and showed him movies of K-State playing and beating the University of Illinois. Roy was impressed. He wasn't big, but was a ferocious adversary and had extremely quick reactions.

Dean Plagge, from a small Kansas town, had also been offered a scholarship to Tulsa University, but he liked K-State basketball. He had been particularly impressed with the team of 1951. One of Tex's assistants, Ernie Barrett, had played on that team.

Larry Fischer, from Pratt, Kansas, had been named to the national high school #1 team in football, but came to K-State wanting to play basketball. Tex recognized his overall athletic ability and offered him a scholarship.

The 1957-58 sophomores looked very promising. Most of them were from Kansas: Glen Long, out of Topeka, had played for Howie Shannon, the assistant coach, in high school. Glen was great on the boards. Wally Frank, from Norton; Jerry Johnson, from Hutchinson; Bill Guthridge, from Parsons; and Steve Douglas and Sonny Ballard, two "townies" from Manhattan. Bob Graham was from Independence, Missouri.

There weren't any players who could have been called hefty or burly. Most were, in fact, probably considered a bit on the lean side, considering their height. They wore short shorts with always-white socks and white high-top canvas Converse shoes. There was no choice about which shoes to wear, and all teams wore the same length shorts. The players' lack of bulk might be attributed to our diets back then (no fast foods), the many miles of walking we put in each day, and the fact that weight-lifting wasn't yet in vogue.

Tex did try the idea of weight lifting on several occasions. The players remember hoisting weights before practices, then returning to the court only to be unable to easily shoot or move their arms.

They abandoned that technique. Muscular strength wasn't as important as endurance in basketball, at least in those days. Another time the coaches decided to try something different and had the players report for a go at cross-country running. That lasted one time as no one saw any real value to that effort, either. In fact, it was learned later that several players hid behind a tree as the group started out and rejoined them as they were returning from the run. Tex settled on conditioning that focused on fundamental training and full court scrimmages.

As the K-State coaches scanned the list of team members they had lined up they surely felt optimistic. They had outstanding players returning, and they had gained some needed height. The schedule would not be an easy one, though. The Big Seven Conference was looking strong, and we were also scheduled to face some tough Big 10 teams. In addition, the schedule included two West coast powers: California, the Pacific Coast Champion; and

1957-58 Team
Top Row: *Howie Shannon, Steve Douglas, Bob Boozer, Jack Parr, Wally Frank, Howie Rice, Larry Fischer, Bill Laude.* **2nd Row:** *Glen Long, Dean Plagge, Bob Graham, Hayden Abbott, Bob Merten, Roy DeWitz, Tex Winter.* **Bottom Row:** *John Stone, Don Matuszak, Don Richards, Sonny Ballard, Jim Holwerda, Bill Guthridge*

Washington, who had tied for second.

Tex remarked about the upcoming games, "You can take a look at our schedule and figure out that either we have a real good basketball team coming up or else we're candidates for the booby hatch!" They would meet four Big 10 teams (including the co-champ, Indiana), perennially competitive Arkansas, and the two Western teams.

In accordance with NCAA rules, the team began practice on October 15th and observers expressed optimism. Tex said everything depended on finding the right combination. He knew they had a chance to field the biggest team in Kansas State history if a certain mix worked. The biggest player was senior Jack Parr, the 6'9" center who had averaged 20.6 points a game last season and been named to the AP and UPI all Big-Seven teams. He had gained Honorable Mention on the All-America designations from the International News Service and Associated Press. Close behind in height was Bob Boozer, a 6'8" junior, also an all Big-Seven selection by the AP and UPI. Bob had averaged 19.6 points a game. Wally Frank, who had performed extremely well as a freshman, matched Bob's height. Other members returning included Bob Merten, 6'3" forward; Don Richards, 6'0" guard; Bill Laude, 6'4" senior forward; and Howie Rice, a 6'8" senior who played both forward and center.

The players were all aware, as Tex had made it clear many times, that no one was assured a starting position, and that effort and skill could vault them over any other team member.

Tex worried that this '57-'58 squad might not be able to match the speed of the previous year's guards. He analyzed the new team's dynamics and came up with this statement: "We should be strong on the boards and have good close-in offense and a good strong bench. We'll be bigger, but we'll also be slower and more conservative. We may find ourselves short on outside shooting. DeWitz and

Ballard are the only two real consistent outside shooters we have as of now. Actually, though, I think the biggest problem is going to be that schedule. It's easily the toughest we have ever tried."

Basketball Magazine predicted that K-State's season would be more frustrating this year than last – "one of the best all-time squads, but they will be forced to play second fiddle to Chamberlain and KU and probably won't be able to beat them." The magazine predicted the possible line up: DeWitz switching from forward to guard, Matuszak as the other guard, rookie Wally Frank at forward, and Boozer and Parr (the 1-2 punch of last season) as forward and center.

Since the Big Seven had voted to include Oklahoma State beginning the next year, this year would be a last shot at the Big Seven title. KU and K-State were considered the top contenders and possibly both would achieve national ranking, but KU had the edge with their 7-foot center, "Wilt the Stilt."

In their first game against the freshman team, Tex started Hayden Abbott, Bob Boozer, Jack Parr, Roy DeWitz, and Don Matuszak. Assistant Coach Howie Shannon commented, "We're satisfied with the progress the freshman team has made." One player, in particular, Cedric Price, who came to K-State on a football scholarship, caught the attention of the crowd with his height and his rebounding skills.

Tex saw definite talent on this new varsity squad, but the right blend of players was still not firm in his mind. It would take the first few games to sense the way the players would come together and use their special talents. He liked to try different mixes of team members, watch the interaction of the players in practice, and trusted that his experience would help him determine the right group. "I plan to keep an open mind," he said, "until the season gets going."

The press and the fans watched anxiously to see if this would be another good team. Good coaching could make a big difference. Could Tex mold this group into a team as good as the one that finished with an 8-4 conference record last year? He certainly seemed to have the ingredients, but could he find the magic mix?

He looked so serious at times as he watched them go through their drills. What made him tick? Just who was this youngest coach in Division I basketball?

***

Morice Fred Winter and his twin sister, Mona Frances, were born in 1922, in Lubbock, Texas. They had an older brother and sister. The brother, Ernest, became a guiding force in Tex's life, enticing him into sports at an early age and urging him into all kinds of competition. Tex was an eager competitor, but because he was small for his age, track and basketball became his best sports. His ability in pole-vaulting in high school would eventually earn him a college scholarship.

Tex Winter's father passed away before Tex reached high school. The family had a hard time making ends meet. Those were dismal years in America's history, and many families were migrating to California to seek better opportunities. His mother decided to move her family to California, following her oldest daughter who was already living there. Ernest, who was finding success in athletics, chose to stay behind in Lubbock. That left Tex "the man of the family" and he soon found a job at a market, taking his pay in day-old vegetables, fruit and bread. This detail proved a lifesaver for the family since his mother's job as a clerk left little money for buying staples. In his spare time Tex hung out at the local playground. It was there that his identity was established, as the kids began calling him "Tex."

Upon entering high school Tex tried out for the basketball team. He captained each of his teams and every year his team won the city championship. A fortuitous event occurred during his senior year when the Loyola basketball team's gym was destroyed and they began working out in a new facility near Tex's home. He was fascinated with the level of play and soon became a regular around the gym, and eventually was designated the "ball boy" for the team. Pete Newell and Phil Woolpert were members of that team and would later become friends and fellow coaches.

Tex went on to play basketball and to vault at Compton Junior College, then accepted a scholarship to Oregon State. It was there that he met his future wife, Nancy Bohnenkamp. This was during WWII, and both Tex and Nancy left school to join the service. Though they ended up in different sections of the country, they stayed in touch and were reunited and married three years later.

Tex trained as a Navy pilot and was also able to participate in sports. As part of his training, he attended both Monmouth College in Illinois and Marquette University in Milwaukee. The latter became a magnet for him and he was later called to coach there.

After his pilot training, Tex became an instructor and it was during this phase that he met and impressed Sam Barry who, in civilian life, was a coach for the USC Trojans. Barry was impressed with Tex's athletic skills and recruited him to play basketball at USC when his enlistment ended. The choice for Tex was easy, since he had already committed to a vaulting scholarship at USC.

It was Sam Barry who recommended Tex for the assistant coaching position at Kansas State. Sam was a friend of head coach Jack Gardner, and when asked about recommendations for the assistant position he named Tex Winter. Gardner was a popular and acclaimed coach who led the Wildcats to some great victories. At age 25, in 1947, Tex became his assistant, and stayed on the job four years before assuming Marquette's head coach position. When

Gardner retired, Tex returned to K-State to take the reins of head coach, in the 1953-54 season.

***

In this 1957-58 season, at 35 years of age, Tex Winter had as his assistants two of K-State's finest former basketball players: Howie Shannon who had played on K-State's 1948 team and been awarded All-American honors; and Ernie Barrett, the freshman coach who had been named to the 2nd team consensus All-America team. Howie, from Monday, Texas, had been recruited after his wartime service to play for Jack Gardner. After school he played several years with the Boston Celtics and then returned to Kansas to coach at a high school in Topeka. Ernie had been a member of the great 1951 team that had gone to the NCAA finals. He, too, had played for the Celtics and was a home grown Kansan, from Wellington.

When October 15th rolled around, the players began their routine for the season. Daily 4-6 p.m. workouts dictated their class schedules. They had to be certain to schedule no class later than 2:00 because after 3:00 they made their way to the gym to be taped, warmed up, and readied for practice by 4:00 p.m. sharp. There they went through fundamentals that Tex emphasized over and over. Tex was an analytical student of the game and had refined an offense he called the "triangle offense." His players had to commit it to memory so they could execute it instinctively. Tex also prepared them to run the fast-break offense that became one of their trademarks. He believed that if a recruit had good athletic skills, a good mind, and was willing to learn, that recruit could become a good player.

Before games the players were restricted to a meal of hot tea and melba toast, no matter what time the games were played. Most games were scheduled on Tuesday and Saturday nights, so the routine on those days was to show up in the afternoon for a scouting report and/or game films, then go home to rest, and report back in time to be taped and warmed up. After games, the training tables offered iced tea, milk, cereal and sandwiches.

First and foremost, Tex was a teacher. He expected discipline and adherence to the rules, and he let the players know that they were primarily students and expected to attend classes and make their grades. He required good deportment, adherence to campus dress and morality codes, and haircuts that were in line with good taste. One player remembers his return to campus in the fall, when he walked down the sidewalk and met the coach who, without a 'hello' or remark about the summer break simply said, "Get a haircut." The players were expected to dress in a suit or sport coat with white shirt and tie for their travel days. Most of the players also donned hats – the standard fedora of that period.

Such a predictable routine was not hard to follow and the players adapted easily. There were no surprise practices, no punishment drills, and no restrictions except "no late nights before games" – particularly on the road. The players soon felt prepared for the beginning of the season.

Basketball was becoming more and more interesting to me as I watched my friend and sometimes-date, Don Matuszak, in scrimmages and games. We had dated several times since the start of school and always had a fun time. I enjoyed seeing him on the court as he scrambled for the ball and partnered with the other guard – Roy DeWitz – in the backcourt.

The official season opener was a home game in Ahearn Fieldhouse against Texas Western. True to predictions, the Wildcats scored a lopsided 76-31 victory. Our big men, Parr and Boozer, led the effort and the bench was emptied early so that everyone got in the game.

Only four days later a talented Indiana University team came to Manhattan and gave the Wildcats a hard-fought contest, but eventually lost by a score of 66-61.

On December 9, the team left Manhattan to play a perennially tough Purdue team on their Indiana court. Again, the Cats prevailed with a final tally of 79-73.

The team's next opponent was Iowa University on December 14 at home. Another victory (86-69), fourth in a row against strong teams, began to draw national attention to the Wildcats. They were ranked 3rd in the country after that game.

In Fayetteville, Arkansas, only two days later, K-State showed their strength again with a 63-48 win.

As the momentum was building for the team, they began to gain recognition from all quarters. Jack Parr was named Favorite Man on Campus, fan clubs for individual players were forming in Kansas and some of the neighboring states, and national attention was starting to focus on the team. In those days, not a lot of college basketball was available on TV so people depended upon newspapers or radio for reports of the games and national rankings.

Basketball was a very different game then. Significant changes have been made in these intervening years. One of the most radical modifications, instituted in 1973, allows freshmen to play on the varsity team. That change opened up more options for coaches. It also gave players the advantage of more spirited competition and the opportunity to develop more fully during their college careers. As we look at statistics in these pages, we must keep in mind that the numbers were incurred over a three, not a four-year period.

One particularly interesting difference about the games of the '50s is that there were no time clocks, which meant lower scoring as well as the familiar strategy of using a slow-tempo to tame teams known for fast breaks or teams that dominated in height. This put the pressure on ball control, usually the responsibility of the guards. Oklahoma State's coach, Hank Iba, was known for using this stalling technique. It placed the onus on the guards in both situations – to control the stall game and to break it up.

The only records that appeared in box scores were for field goals, free throws, and rebounds. No mention was made of assists or steals, which could often change the pace and score of the game. Actual minutes of time played by each member were also not listed in the statistics.

A big evolution occurred in the early 1980s when the three-point basket was introduced. That gave more empowerment to the guards and the shorter players. Before then we had only the two-point basket, which tended to make it more of a "feed the big men" game, especially when a team had a height advantage. The outside shot was more of a risk, so it made sense to get the ball into the deep post. Tall men were those over 6' 6" and there weren't that many of them in the game in the '50s. Also, probably because of the risk of injury, dunking the ball was taboo.

In that 1957-58 season, the Wildcats were enjoying some very decisive victories. Tex seemed to have adjusted his lineup to a pretty stable group. Generally he started Boozer, Parr, Abbott, DeWitz, and Matuszak. He sought out Glen Long when it came to rebounding and Fischer when he needed muscle under and around the basket. Holwerda was a good shooting guard from outside and came in to relieve the starters. Sophomore Wally Frank was showing signs of becoming a standout forward, so Tex often used him.

As the holiday season approached Tex had every reason to be proud and optimistic, with the expectation that his now nationally ranked 3rd place team could go far – if they could just overcome KU. Behind the scenes, though, some dark clouds were building – clouds seen only by the most scrutinizing observers. Things were not as happy go lucky as they appeared on the court, but most of the players knew nothing about what was happening.

The story is a hard one to tell, for those involved did not talk publicly, then or now. (Remember that these were radically different times; our country was a long way yet from these tell-all gossipy days we're familiar with now.) For the players and coaches who did have a sense of what was happening, the overriding instinct was to keep quiet – protect the team. The players who caught some inkling of undercurrents did not ask questions. The narrative will never be fully explained, nor will we attempt to probe the details here.

Some of the players had noticed that Jack Parr did not always show up for practice, and that when he did he sometimes left early or practiced alone, apart from the group. Occasionally the team doctor, Dr. Cooper, was present, but that wasn't considered unusual since Doc was an avid basketball fan. The team simply assumed that Jack was having some troubles with classes, or that he practiced alone because he was working on a new shot, or that he just didn't feel sociable. The players refrained from discussing Parr's isolation, but it was becoming a distraction at times.

Jack was a big man from Virginia who, as a rule, was fairly quiet. He had literally dropped from the blue into the lineup. Tex had never seen him play. Another recruit, Bill Laude, had met Parr at a sports summer camp. Bill contacted Tex to tell him about the impressive 6'9" player, and reported that Parr had not been talking to Division I schools – that his college decision was still up in the air. Tex *was* interested. He asked Bill to have Jack call him if he would like to talk and Jack did call. With only two years of high school experience, Jack was excited about joining this Division I team and the group that Tex was putting together at K-State. He proved to be a very good rebounder and a good scorer, and continued to improve his game in his three years at K-State. In this '57-58 season he was a senior.

In December the team faced some big games. The Athletic Directors from K-State and KU had decided to host a double header – shortly before Christmas – called the Sunflower Classic. The two teams would not play each other, but would alternate courts and foes on successive nights. Because the plan featured some of the nation's top-ranked teams and players, the directors figured they had hit upon a terrific marketing strategy. On the first night, on the K-State court, Kansas would play the University of California, while Kansas State faced off against Washington University. The next night they would swap places and play the other visiting teams.

Tex talked eagerly about what his team could do with strong adversaries. He stated that, offensively, some of his starters hadn't yet come up to expectations. He said he was referring to Jack Parr, who had hit so well last year but was off to a slow start this season; Roy DeWitz, who also had had some trouble in the early stages; and Hayden Abbott, who had not reached the peak he had achieved as a sophomore, perhaps because of continuing back problems. Don Matuszak, Tex said, also had not been shooting. He valued Matuszak as a playmaker who helped others score, but wanted him to begin shooting so the defense wouldn't drop back on the others.

Crowds were expected, but nothing like the explosion of fans that filled Ahearn. Students that usually went home during this time stayed in town. Fans from all corners flocked to the exhibition – the largest crowd that had ever fit into Ahearn: 15,500. When it was all over, both Kansas teams had won their games, proof that they had earned their national rankings. (See Sunflower Classic.)

The much anticipated Big Eight 1957 pre-season tournament, scheduled as usual in Kansas City, was to begin right after Christmas – December 27-31, only six days after the Sunflower Classic. Fans from both Kansas schools saw this as a pitting of their teams against one another in the same arena, and were much aware of the significance. The action was to take place in the Municipal Auditorium in downtown Kansas City, with KU the predicted victor in the duel. (Oklahoma State, the 8th team to enter the Big 7, was not scheduled to compete this year, so Princeton held the last spot.)

K-State students saved their money to go over to the tournament. Many had families there or knew someone who did, so there was a large contingent from our school to cheer our team. Don and I were now dating fairly frequently but I wasn't able to afford the trip. At home, though, I listened to all the games on the radio. My mother and grandmother, who had both suddenly developed an interest in basketball, were usually there beside me. I loved teasing my grandmother about her close following of the team. She even insisted once that her ladies' circle of card players keep the radio on during a particular game. At the end of the contest, the scores of the winner and loser were announced. They had been tuned in to the wrong game – been listening to a UNLV game! My grandmother defended herself by saying, "Well, that one boy had a funny sounding name and I thought they were trying to say Matuszak!"

In the first round, Kansas handily beat Oklahoma, 68-50, and went on to face Iowa State, the victor over Colorado, 81-48. KU's subsequent win over Iowa State, with Wilt Chamberlain scoring 27 points, put them in the finals. Kansas State, in the other bracket, handled Missouri in the first round, 60-54, then went on to play Nebraska, the winner over Princeton, 74-64. Kansas State won big over Nebraska, 88-57, earning them a spot in the finals against KU – as most of us had foreseen.

The semi-finals were a cakewalk for the Wildcats. In the last 11 minutes alone, the Cats put in 25 points to Nebraska's 9. The Wildcats hit 46.3% from the field, while the Huskers could manage just 37.1%. K-State showed balanced scoring with Boozer putting in 18 points, Abbott with 15, DeWitz with 14, Parr, 12, and Frank, 11. Others scoring were Guthridge with six, Matuszak four, Long three, Ballard and Laude each two, and Rice with one. The Cats fielded 12 players before game's end. Then it was on to the last game!

The game was billed as the "big showdown" – the game that would set the precedent for the remainder of the season. Both Kansas teams had unblemished records to date, nine wins with no losses. Kansas State had the tall men around the basket, but KU had Wilt, who could score from anywhere near the goal and was intimidating with his 7' stature. It was the battle that sportswriters had predicted, the one between the Big Bopper (Wilt) and Big Bob (Boozer).

FINALS: BIG 8 PRE-SEASON TOURNAMENT
@ KANSAS CITY
12/27/57-12/31/57

When game time arrived, two of K-State's star players had the flu. Hayden Abbott never made it into the game; Bob Boozer tried and lasted through the first half, scoring only nine points. It seemed apparent then that the Cats' strategy was to concentrate as much on the other players as on Chamberlain. The plan didn't pay off; the 7-footer had one of his best nights with a total 38 points and 18 rebounds. Ron Loneski, KU forward, played a remarkable game and had 16 points and took down 16 rebounds. The Cats averaged just 30% on their field goals. Jack Parr was hampered by four fouls in the first half, and fouled out with 8:03 left in the 2nd half. The Cats couldn't catch up. The KU Jayhawks took the victory and tournament championship by a score of 79-65. Wally Frank was high point man for the Wildcats with 18, DeWitz had 16, and Parr hit for 11. Boozer scored nine, Long six, Matuszak three, and Richards two.

Two players on the KU team made the All-Tournament team: Wilt, who was the unanimous choice for outstanding player; and his teammate, Ron Loneski. The K-State players that made the team were Roy DeWitz and Bob Boozer. Lyle Frahm from Iowa State rounded out the five.

***

January, 1958. We soon saw that our players had become more of a team – seemed to be learning one another's strengths and weaknesses. Parr, Boozer, and Frank had the height, so Tex urged the others to get the ball inside if at all possible. He often stood at the sideline gesturing frantically with a repetitive hand motion and yelling to the guards, "Move it, move it!" DeWitz and Matuszak seemed to read each other well in running the offense. Some remember Tex yelling at the guards, "Don't shoot! Don't shoot!" If they did and the ball went in, he quietly just said, "Nice shot." The players were all skilled in initiating a fast break or running the half court offense. When the defense on the big guys sagged, they fanned the ball out to the guards for attempted outside shots.

The guys spent about three hours together in the gym each day, sometimes more when they were on the road or on game days. They got to know and like one another and loved to humorously spar and tease back and forth. They dined together, for the training table in the stadium was the facility that served three meals a day just to the athletes (with the exception of Sunday when only breakfast and a large midday meal was served). The food bonanza was part of every athlete's scholarship provision. They ate well, and they ate ravenously. A favorite story told about their appetites centered on Roy DeWitz. He had come to school as a 5'11" freshman weighing around 135 pounds, and started his sophomore year at a bit over 6'3" and around 185 pounds. Roy was the youngest of ten children, a fact that made you wonder if the training table's abundance of food caused his unusual growth spurt. When Tex talked to groups or new recruits, he liked to indicate just that.

An athletic scholarship included room and board, plus fees and books. The guys were paid $15/month, or $1 an hour, for 15 hours of an assigned job on campus. That was their "laundry" money, but they had to work for it. The jobs included stocking and distributing uniforms at the ROTC, officiating at intra-mural games, working for a professor, and delivering food and drinks to those in the press box during football games.

Some of the players roomed together. Part of the stadium contained a dorm. Other players were scattered around the campus in basement apartments or fraternity houses.

One of the roommate pairings was unusual for that time, but not unusual on our campus: Boozer, the only black player on the team, roomed with Matuszak, a white player from a very segregated suburb of Chicago. Another freshman player also lived in their small room in West Stadium that contained the bare necessities – two bunk beds and three desks. There was barely room for a footlocker at the end of the beds. Across the hall and under the stadium seats were lockers. Two people shared a locker, which consisted of a chest of drawers and a small space for hanging clothes. In those times there was no such thing as wash-and-wear clothing, so almost everything you wore needed to be on a hanger. The lockers were kept locked, so to get dressed a player had to cross the hall, unlock the space, and retrieve his clothes for the day.

On January 6th, Minnesota University came to play. And did they play! They almost took home the victory, but K-State won by one point, 72-71.

On January 11th the Wildcats began their regular conference schedule and defeated Nebraska, 74-59, in Manhattan, Kansas.

The Wildcats demonstrated their cohesiveness again on January 18th when they played Oklahoma in Manhattan. Both teams were ranked: K-State at #2 and Oklahoma at #14. Although behind at halftime, K-State won at the buzzer: 64-60.

One week later, the Cats faced Iowa State. The Cyclones had always played against us very well and in this game they had the home-court advantage. Again, the Wildcats prevailed with a 65-54 win. They had scrambled through the conference so far, unbeaten.

West Virginia remained one of the few unbeaten major college teams and, as such, was #1 in the polls for the fourth successive week. They had received 69 of the 104 first place votes, outnumbering everyone else in the race. On a basis of ten points for first place, nine points for second place, etc., West Virginia had compiled an impressive 941 points. Second was Kansas State with only four firsts and 590 points. Kansas University was right behind with 586 points, but had received six firsts. San Francisco was in fourth place and Cincinnati was fifth.

K-State was now leading the conference with a 3-0, but would have to put that record on the line twice in rapid-fire succession. On Saturday February 1, they were to play at home against Colorado, and the following Monday meet their main rival – at KU's arena. Tex called the recent win against Iowa State "our best full game of the season," but pointed out that "we've had plenty of time to prepare for the three conference games to date, with a week to get ready for each one. Now we have to face Colorado here on Saturday, then scramble to get braced for Kansas."

"I feel, however," he said, "that we showed good poise and playmaking at Iowa State. That doesn't leave as many problems as we might have had. For the full 40 minutes we looked better than we have looked before this season." Tex was usually controlled and rather stoic when he talked to reporters or booster clubs. He never used a rah-rah approach to or about his team. He analyzed and scrutinized and gave his assessment. He went on to say he saw no reason to change the lineup from the five "old reliables" who had become fixtures. Boozer had hit a shooting slump against Iowa State, ending with only four points in the game, his lowest in two seasons of play. But his rebounding and all-around play were as polished as ever, according to Tex Winter. "Boozer is a great guy and a great basketball player. We expect him to bounce back against Colorado and Kansas."

Even in his "slump," Boozer was currently leading the Cats with his 18.1 points a game. Next was Jack Parr with a 13.8 average. Showing the scoring balance, three other regulars were hitting at nine points or better. Roy DeWitz, the senior guard, had put in 18 points against Iowa State and was averaging 9.6. Forwards Hayden Abbott and Wally Frank were both averaging 9.0. Don Matuszak, the junior guard, had the lowest average with a 6.4, but Winter explained that as a "case of shyness." Tex added, "Don hesitates to fire away from outside. He doesn't shoot as much as we'd like him to since he doesn't feel he hits well enough, yet Don is our third best shooter at this point. He's hitting a good 41%."

Boozer and Matuszak liked to constantly needle each other about their shooting. Bob would ridicule Don's flat shot that he'd take from outside. Because Don had worked in high school to supplement his family's income, he had only been able to play ball his last year in high school. In those years before, when he did have a chance to play, it was usually in some town arena with a low ceiling, so his shot had little arc. He prided himself, though, on making 104 points in one town game. Of course, the teasing was always double-edged: Boozer knew he would get it back. Don liked to remind Bob that every time he threw the ball into the deep post to Boozer, it never came out! Their repartee was endless and infectious. The other players joined in the fun.

Colorado had suffered two league losses to Kansas and Oklahoma and had a 5-8 record in all games. "Colorado is strong enough to hand any team a loss," Winter said. "They have proved that by beating Iowa State and scaring Kansas." Colorado had indeed led through most of the first half of their game with KU.

"Our big problem" Winter added, "is that we have to go all out to tune our game for Colorado, and then, two nights later, we meet an entirely different style of play with Kansas. It's a big order."

Against Colorado, the Cats had swept both games the previous season and had a 16-6 advantage in their series. However, Kansas had a lopsided margin of victories, 90-44, against K-State in their total games. Both teams could be dangerous.

On the 1st of February, the Colorado Buffaloes roamed to Manhattan and the Wildcats exploded in a win of 83-54. That game proved to many that K-State was for real. The Cats shot 50% from the field and 70% from the line. Their ranking, nationally, was back to #3. The next big step was against Wilt and KU.

The Wildcat statistics, posted in early February, showed the team's six regulars averaging 40% from the field and 65.5% from the line. Tex felt that they could do well down the stretch if they could at least hold those figures or, hopefully, better them.

	FG%	FT%	Rebounds	Points
Boozer	45	70	183	19.6
Parr	34	62	192	14.4
Abbott	39	49	100	9.6
DeWitz	31	78	109	8.8
Frank	52	69	70	8.4
Matuszak	42	65	67	6.4

Vs. KANSAS UNIVERSITY (2/3/58)
@ LAWRENCE

Going into this game, KU held the national ranking of #2 and K-State was now at #4. The two main men on the respective squads were Bob Boozer with his 19 points a game against Wilt Chamberlain, who was averaging 32 points per game.

It was billed as the "championship game" or "duel of the year," but whatever anyone called it, no one was disappointed. It was all the fans could ask for: a real hard-fought match with two of the best teams in the country. Kansans, particularly, were on the edge of their seats. The sportswriters waited anxiously.

Tex had a plan in mind and that was to keep "the Big Dipper" Chamberlain hemmed in by placing Parr between Wilt and the basket and Boozer fronting Wilt. DeWitz played man-to-man on Loneski and Abbott and Matuszak zoned the other three players. In doing so, Tex hoped to keep both Chamberlain's scoring and rebounding down and force him into fouls and off-target shooting.

The Wildcats got off to a fast start and led by ten points through much of the first half. At intermission they had a 41-28 lead. Near the end, however, with three and a half minutes to go, a Kansas rally put them in the lead for the first time. The score was 58-56.

The fired-up Wildcat team kept up their intensity and Boozer and Parr hemmed Wilt in most of the time, allowing him only 25 points. DeWitz contributed to the battle under the basket by out-rebounding Wilt, the first time that had been accomplished since Wilt began playing as a sophomore. DeWitz, 9" shorter than Chamberlain, gathered in 15 rebounds to Wilt's 14.

Boozer exploded with every kind of shot, scoring a total of 32 points. He made the basket that tied the score at 60-60 at the end of regulation play and, in the end of the first overtime, he again hit the crucial shot that tied the score. Parr made two great blocks on shots by Chamberlain during the overtime period and the Wildcats went ahead in the second overtime to win by a score of 79-75!

Both teams hit an average of 43% from the field, but the Wildcats decided the game at the free throw line. K-State hit 21 of 26 while the Jayhawks hit only 13 of 24.

Parr scored 15 points, Abbott 13, Matuszak eight, Frank six, and DeWitz five.

The fantastic victory put the Cats in first place in the conference and almost assured them the title. Winter said after the game: "K-State may not have the finesse of a lot of ball clubs, but this is undoubtedly one of the best Wildcat teams in the history of the school." He explained again their defensive strategy, and said with a smile, "The league race is not over yet, but we have a jump on them!"

Sports Illustrated, in their assessment of the game, said Tex Winter did not have to worry about his second-guessers, that the most rabid fans could hardly have asked for a better effort, and Winter could not have expected better execution of his plans. KU's coach, Dick Harp, (the magazine said) was undoubtedly in for a rough time from those who doubted his coaching ability. "He does not deserve it. Kansas was beaten by a better one, one which may well be the *best in the nation*."

Kansas State accomplished three things by beating KU in that important Big Seven game. They showed that Kansas – even with Wilt – could be beaten; they made it virtually impossible for any other team in the conference to capture the title; and they boosted their national ranking the following week to number one in the nation.

In the Associated Press rankings (with votes from sportswriters and broadcasters), the Wildcats barely edged out West Virginia. Of 108 ballots Kansas State got only 32 first place votes to West Virginia's 43, but the votes for second, third, and fourth places, which had previously gone to many teams, now swung toward the Wildcats. The point totals were Kansas State with 878 and West Virginia with 865. Kansas University, with 27 first place votes the week before, received only one vote for first that week and slid down to fourth place. Cincinnati remained in third place with 730 points and San Francisco and Oklahoma State were fifth and sixth.

Tex had done what he'd set out to do: win the victory over KU the K-State way, with no gimmicks or trick plays. He had given Parr and Boozer the job of defending Wilt, and set his other players to contain the rest of the squad. He relied on his team's great fast break, an offensive strength they used frequently. He had also counted on his team's intense desire to win, plus the enthusiasm of the Wildcat fans. Oklahoma's coach, Doyle Parrack, called those fans the most spirited group he'd ever seen.

The K-State student body loved the team, the coach, the victories, and the national acclaim. The team's success was the topic of conversation in every corner of the state. Those "boys," as they were then called, became the dragon-slayers, the astronauts, the heroes of our time. Very few people, however, knew that one of the super heroes had a problem – a problem no one discussed, one that progressed as the year proceeded. A few team members were not even aware that there was any difficulty. The coach and the team doctor were confronting the situation, and they concurred that whatever was causing Jack Parr's troubles would only worsen if he were removed from the stability of the team.

Sometime that following week a photograph was hastily shot showing the regular starting line-up – Boozer, Parr, Abbott, DeWitz, and Matuszak – along with Tex, behind a "Number 1" sign. Unfortunately, the picture was premature, and it left out the "regular sixth player," Wally Frank. The picture also omitted the ones on the bench that Tex counted on in every game, those who were ready with fierce determination every time he called upon them.

Throughout the years, that picture has haunted K-State's basketball history, sustaining the belief that the 1957-58 team achieved the final ranking as number one in the nation. The true facts went askew with that one quick photo, made in celebration of the defeat of their arch-rival, KU. It is true that for that week the national ranking put the team at the top of the heap. Soon thereafter, though, the team began to slide.

On the plus side, the semester was over and there was not one casualty in the grades department. Tex had always emphasized that the players were there for a college education and had to achieve a balance between schooling and basketball. If they had trouble, they were to let the coaches know. Steve Douglas headed the grades, to no one's surprise. His teammates sometimes referred to him as "the Senator" or "the Professor."

Others had nicknames, too. Matuszak was known as "Tooze," or as "Rat," the latter given to him by Boozer when he discovered that their room had mice because of some goodies Don received from home and left unwrapped. Boozer began referring to their room as "the rat's nest." This proved another "gotcha" for Boozer and he continued from then on to use the nickname, which was adopted by the rest of the team. The fans chanted "Booze…Booze…Booze" when Bob was on a hot streak, so that was the name the players used for him. Glen Long was called "Snakey" or "Snake" because of his ability to sneak in for rebounds. Abbott was called "Skeebo" or "Skee," for some unknown reason. Bill Guthridge was usually called "Billy." Sonny Ballard was "Red" for his carrot-colored hair, and the players yelled "Waldene" to Wally Frank – his given name.

On February 8th, only three days after the KU victory, the Wildcats defeated Iowa State 77-70, in a home game that toppled several records. (See game.) A week later they traveled to Colorado and came home with another win, 68-62, in a tough battle in Boulder.

With a 17-1 record, the Wildcats had given Coach Winter his best record in his five seasons as head coach. (The Cats in 1955-56 had won 17 games, and took the conference crown, but they ended with a 17-8 season.) Now our team had only two remaining road games left: February 22nd with Missouri and March 3rd with Nebraska.

K-State had beaten Missouri in pre-season play, 69-51, but in their long-time series, Missouri held a 56-46 edge. In the conference so far, Missouri posted a 3-5 record and a 9-9 in all games.

Tex placed equal value on each of the five remaining games. "They all count the same in the standings and we could be beat by any of our remaining opponents," he cautioned. "It's reasonable to assume there are some surprises left." When asked if the Wildcats' number one rating had any effect, Winter replied, "I don't think so. It certainly hasn't made the players cocky. We feel that it gives us something to live up to. I think the biggest difference the top rating has made is that it keys up all our opponents for their games with us. They are zeroing in on our game, fired up to the maximum, for the chance to knock over the nation's top team."

Winter went on to give credit to the rest of the conference teams. "We are giving maximum effort in every game. It's a real credit to our opponents and to our Big Seven basketball that most games are decided by narrow margins. As I have said before, this is a league where any team on a given night can beat any other team."

The Cat's journey to Columbia, Missouri, netted them a victory of 82-61, enabling them to hold on to the #1 spot, but they just barely edged out West Virginia who had the most first place votes (22). The Wildcats received 17 votes and Cincinnati 14. In fourth place was San Francisco, and Temple came in fifth. Kansas had slid down to 10th place.

The Wildcats were undefeated in eight league games, so mathematically all contenders were out of the race. Kansas had suffered its second straight upset, a loss to Iowa State, 48-42. The Jayhawks' record in the league now stood at 6-4 and they still had two remaining games.

And, K-State clinched it!! With a final score of 68-51 over Oklahoma on February 25th, Kansas State claimed the champion crown! The victory coincided with Coach Tex Winter's 36th birthday. He said it was the best present he could have asked for. "If anyone had told me before the season started that we would have the championship won with three games remaining, I would have suggested they have their head examined. Winning nine in a row in this conference is almost an unbelievable feat." The Wildcats held an overall 19-1 record, their only defeat to KU in the holiday tournament.

Winter praised Bob Boozer for his outstanding rebounding and defense in the second half of the game. The coach would not comment on the team's chances in the tournament. More than likely it would be a contest with Cincinnati, as they were the favorite in the Missouri Valley league. Doyle Parrack, the OU coach, said this about K-State: "Let's put it this way. They're not overrated. I hope they win it. Man for man they are the best team we have ever played."

In the late part of February, the Wildcats had held on to their averages. Statistics released at that time showed the starting six with 41% of field goals and 67% from the free throw line.

	FG%	FT%	Rebounds	Points
Boozer	45	74	236	20.5
Parr	35	63	216	14.7
Abbott	37	53	118	8.7
DeWitz	31	78	129	7.8

Frank	50	67	98	8.0
Matuszak	48	67	78	7.0

Kansas State was, by no means, finding it easy to be conference champions. They had stepped onto a battleground. Against fierce resistance they had to prove their number one ranking. On March 1st in the skirmish with Missouri, fighting between players broke out and K-State's Glen Long and the Tigers' Glenn Forristall were banished from the game before intermission. Throughout the first period there was also a verbal battle between Tex and the other coach, Sparky Stalcup. Tex sometimes second-guessed an official's call, but it was out of character for him to have an argument with an opposing coach.

Playing without center Jack Parr, Bob Boozer took up the slack and scored 35 points to lead the scoring and the Wildcats maintained control of the game all the way. They hit a hot 52.6% of their shots from the field and 73% from the charity line. Wally Frank, who had started in Parr's place, was impressive and led in rebounding with 12 as he scored 14 points. Also in the scoring column were Matuszak with 13, Fischer 10, Long and Douglas four each, and Bill Laude and Roy DeWitz two each. The Wildcats, in this game on their home court with very enthusiastic and spirited fans, were glad to claim the victory with a score of 86-75.

Only two days later on March 3rd, again playing without Parr, K-State played Nebraska pretty evenly throughout the first half, but was down by 21-24 going into the halftime. Boozer, who scored the Wildcats' first 12 points, had 17 at the half, but was charged by then with three fouls.

Nebraska managed to break through the K-State defense in the early minutes of the second half and took a 33-24 lead. By then Boozer had been charged with his fourth foul. He got his final one with the score at 40-30 and 8:30 to go in the game. From that point on, Nebraska coasted to an easy win with a 15-point lead at one point. The final score was 55-48. K-State was stunned.

It was a huge letdown for the team, even though they had won the conference title. The Wildcats had shot only 31% from the field and 76% from the charity line, while Nebraska hit 57% of their field goals, but only 55% of their free throws. Boozer led the scoring with 20 points. Fischer, hitting 4 out of 6 from the field and 2 for 2 from the line, had 10. Frank had eight, Abbott four, and Ballard, Long, and Matuszak each had two. Both Boozer and Matuszak fouled out.

In a dismal last game of the regular schedule, K-State lost to rival KU by a score of 61-44, its only loss on their home court during the season. Unfortunately, this was their second straight loss, having just been defeated by Nebraska the week before.

K-State was out-played in almost every department as the Jayhawks jumped off to an 8-0 lead. The Wildcats had their coldest hitting of the season, shooting 19 of 71 shots for a 26.8% while KU's average was 37.7%. The Jayhawks out-rebounded the Cats 50-37 with Chamberlain taking down 15 for the high. Wilt was also the high scorer of the game with 23 points. Roy DeWitz led the Cats with 11. Boozer scored ten, Frank nine, Matuszak six, Parr four, and Abbott and Holwerda two each.

KU's victory gave them a tie for second place in the conference as they finished with an 8-4 mark.

"I don't remember us playing any worse," said Winter. "The only thing we did was try. We got off to a slow start and were behind the eight-ball all the way. The game was lost in the first ten minutes." He summed up the situation this way: "The season ended for us two weeks ago when we won the championship and we've been flat ever since. The NCAA should give us more incentive. I hope it will be a new season for us. There ought to be a lot more hustle in practice and our physical condition will be good if Parr can stay healthy."

It was an exciting and tense week for the Wildcats as they prepared for what would probably be their biggest battles of the season. Four teams, all of them outstanding nationally, would face off in the regional contest in Lawrence, Kansas. Second-ranked Cincinnati had the nation's leading scorer in Oscar Robertson. He was averaging 34.5 points a game and the team had an average of 86.3 points. Tex knew Oscar would be hard to stop, but was optimistic: "I don't know how we'll stop Robertson but I expect our boys to be in the ball game all the way. Boozer and Parr did a good job on Wilt and I'm just hoping they handle Robertson in the same manner."

The other two teams in the regionals were Oklahoma State, ranked second in the nation defensively, and Arkansas – co-champions of the Southwest Conference. Iba said of his Oklahoma State Cowboys, "We are not too deep and lack a strong big man, but we've made 47% of our shots this season." Arkansas coach, Glen Rose, expressed his optimism, "I know we didn't start the season too well, but we've come along fast. Don't count us out."

The double-header would feature Arkansas against Oklahoma State and Cincinnati vs. Kansas State in the first round.

REGIONALS (3/14/58)
@ LAWRENCE, KS
Vs. CINCINNATI

In one of the most exciting games of the season, the two All-Americans, Big O (Oscar Robertson) and Big B (Bob Boozer) led their teams into the big face-off. It turned out to be a battle to the finish line, not only once, but twice.

Boozer carried the Cats' offense in the opening minutes, getting lots of help through Parr's screening out of Connie Dierking, Cincy's 6'10" giant. Parr dominated the boards and pulled in 12 rebounds, while Dierking had only five. Oscar scored 18 points in the first half, but didn't have another field goal until 12:40 had elapsed in the second half. The teams left at the half with Cincinnati ahead by one point, 40-39.

In the second half Wally Frank got a hot hand and Roy DeWitz, who had gone scoreless in the entire first half, got down to serious business. Roy started hitting and swished some great outside shots through the net. The score was tied six times and finally came down to a last shot. K-State was leading, 74-73, when Robertson was fouled by Boozer in the most disputed call of the game. Robertson was going in for the basket and was being defended by Boozer. The predictable clash resulted in a foul call against Boozer. There was one second on the clock.

The 6'5" Oscar had a chance to put his team ahead by one point with his two free shots at the line. Taking his time he hit the first one to tie the game at 74-all. Then, this sophomore, who was playing one of the most important games he'd ever played, took his time walking the length of the court, rubbing his hands and shaking them. He returned to the line and missed the second shot.

The overtime started without Dierking in the Cincy lineup as he had fouled out with ten seconds left in the regular game. The first shot was by the Bearcats' Mendenhall, making the score 76-74, with 4:35 on the clock. The Wildcats got the ball and lost control of it, giving Oscar an opportunity to drive for the baseline. Boozer was waiting and Robertson was called for charging, his third such foul and his fifth overall. That put him out of the game, but he had scored 30 points.

Boozer hit one of his free throws to bring the Wildcats within one, 76-75, and four minutes remaining. Cincinnati's Davis made a layup for a 78-75 lead. Then DeWitz began his rally. With 2:25 left he hit one from 30 feet and the Wildcats were behind only 78-77. Mendenhall raced down the court for what looked like a sure basket but Parr jumped high and pushed it back at him and K-State got possession with 1:28 left.

DeWitz fired again from 30 feet and hit it, putting K-State ahead with a score of 79-78. Fischer, a very proven reserve, then fouled with 51 seconds on the clock, but Cincy's Ron Dykes missed both. Jim Holwerda was fouled with 30 seconds and he hit one for an 80-78 score. With 16 seconds left, Cincinnati threw the ball out of bounds, then fouled DeWitz. He hit another for 81-78. The Bearcats weren't finished. Davis made a long jump shot with three seconds to go, making it 81-80. DeWitz gained control of the ball and was again fouled with one second left. He hit both shots for an 83-80 score. Although the Bearcats called a timeout, it was hopeless. Their strategy of rolling the ball down the court didn't pay off as there was no time to do anything. The buzzer went off and the Wildcats rejoiced.

Oscar was high scorer for the game, with 30 points, and his teammate Connie Dierking had 18. Boozer held the high of 24 for the Wildcats, Parr scored 17, DeWitz 15, Frank 12, Matuszak nine, Fischer five, and Holwerda one. Boozer and Robertson each had 14 rebounds. K-State's Parr had 12, DeWitz pulled in nine, Frank had five, Matuszak four, and Abbott and Fischer two each.

REGIONALS (3/15/58)
Vs. OKLAHOMA STATE

Shooting a torrid 55%, the Wildcats were decisive on both offense and defense against the Oklahoma State Cowboys. Bob Boozer showed why he was an All-American candidate as he hit 12 from the field and added two free throws for the game high of 26 points. Don Matuszak, though, proved to be the best shooter of the night, putting in six of seven from the field and two for two from the line, scoring a total of 14 points. Parr, who had fed Don as he went in for driving layups, scored 13 points and snared ten rebounds.

The Cats were ahead 38-31 at the half, but Oklahoma State brought it up to 38-34 before the Wildcats took over. Wally Frank hit five straight points in the rally, putting the score at 50-38 with only 13 minutes left. K-State kept Oklahoma State restricted to free throws for the next four minutes as they brought the score to 61-41. Then, with less than five minutes to go, Coach Winter removed his starters, and the fans – most of them from K-State – went wild.

Arlen Clark, Oklahoma State's big center, scored 24 points, and the only other teammate to score in double figures was Jerry Hale who had 11. The Cowboys took the same amount of shots from the field as the Wildcats, but could only manage to average 33% while the Wildcats put in an impressive 55%. The final score: 69-57.

Starters for K-State were Abbott, Boozer, Parr, DeWitz, and Matuszak. The other Wildcats in the scoring column, not mentioned above, were Frank with ten and DeWitz with six.

The scene back in Aggieville was total exuberance. Fans who had stayed home started a bonfire in an intersection of the little town. Damage was kept to a minimum, however, as students got the word that the team would be coming back soon; they wanted to greet their team upon its arrival back on campus. The Cats were only about an hour and a half away, so the crowd streamed to the field house to cheer the players upon return and, hopefully, to hear from Coach Winter and the players themselves. The team obliged and returned to a huge crowd of faithful Wildcat fans. Tex spoke to the crowd and, after some rousing cheers, the rally ended because curfew had already been broken.

But the students weren't finished celebrating. They manned the phones the next day and night and organized a mass walkout for Monday. Blockades were put in place early that morning – in a spirit of goodwill – and professors and students were turned away from classes. President James McCain, an extremely well-liked man who was nearly always supportive of the students, tried to sway them from taking a day away from classes. He appealed to the student council in an emergency meeting but, in the end, realized his argument was getting nowhere, so gave his quiet okay. The day would be made up during Easter vacation. President McCain even attended the jubilant assembly that afternoon when the team and the crowd came together once again. It was a dignified yet rousing affair, and each player gave a short speech. The crowd cheered until their throats were hoarse. Coach Winter thanked the crowd for their support, pointing out the importance of that support to the team's success, and officially called "Wildcat Day" to a conclusion.

***

Oscar Robertson and K-State's Bob Boozer were unanimous choices for the Midwest Regional All-Tournament team. Also selected were Jack Parr and Roy DeWitz from K-State, and Arlen Clark from Oklahoma State.

Then, onward to the NCAA championships in Louisville, Kentucky. The four teams that had survived their regionals and earned the right to play for the title were Seattle, Temple, Kentucky, and Kansas State. Speculation was that Cincinnati had been one of the strongest teams in the nation and any team that could beat them could very well come out on top. At least, that's what K-State fans wanted to believe.

The truth was that anything could happen on any given night, a truth proven again and again in the game of basketball. Sportswriters and prognosticators agreed that Kansas State had some extremely solid points in their favor. First, the towering combination of Bob Boozer, Jack Parr, and Wally Frank: not many teams had that array of shooting talent and height. Just as important was the fine outside combination of Roy DeWitz and Don Matuszak. They not only moved the ball deceptively, they could also hit. And if the tall men were screened out, the guards had the ability to either aim for the hoop or to lob in over the defense to one of the big guys. Parr, after some late-season troubles, seemed to be back at peak performance. And Boozer, who had made the prestigious selection of All-American, was looking ready. Hayden Abbott had an injured finger that would hopefully be healed by the play-offs but if it wasn't, Wally Frank was no drop-off in effectiveness. Also, Frank added height to the mix.

K-State's ability to control or at least dominate the boards was also a key factor. In regular season, opponents averaged only 60.2 points a game. Boozer had averaged 20 points a game over the season and made 50 points during the two regional play-off games. While it was easy to consider the importance of the big men, DeWitz and Matuszak had scored 44 points in those regional games, just shy of 1/3 of the 152 total.

This looked like a solid ball club, and for the first time since 1951 they were in a position to take K-State's first-ever NCAA championship. Odds-makers were picking K-State to take home the ultimate prize. Kentucky, the Southeastern Conference champion, was the veteran of the tournament, having won three titles in ten appearances. Kentucky was the obvious second choice. Temple, from the Middle Atlantic Conference, had won 23 straight games and was given 3-1 odds. Seattle, the "at large" team that featured All-American player Elgin Baylor, came in with 9-2 odds.

Snow delayed arrival for some of the teams, but all were able to practice on the Friday afternoon before the double-header. The first game featured Kentucky versus Temple in the opener and K-State against Seattle in the later game. The winners would battle on the following night for the crown.

A look at team and individual scoring for the final four teams showed them pretty evenly matched in scoring. Seattle was ahead in the category, averaging 80.9 while Kentucky had 74.9, Temple with a 73.9, and K-State averaging 70.5. Temple gave fewer points to their opponents with their 58.4 average, K-State with 60.4, Kentucky had 62.4, and Seattle averaged 68.6.

Elgin Baylor from Seattle led all scorers with his 33.1 average, and only one other teammate had an average in the double figures. Kentucky had a balanced effort with four players in double figures. K-State's Bob Boozer had 20.4 and Jack Parr, 14.3. Temple's Guy Rodgers averaged 20.1, and three of his teammates averaged in double digits.

In analyzing team strengths, one report pointed out that the K-State team had what it took in all categories, including grades. No one on the 15-member squad had failed a single hour during the fall semester. Top man was Steve Douglas with his 2.6 (on the 3.0 system). The GPA of the squad was 1.56.

Tex decided to depart from the usual starting lineup for the game, putting in Wally Frank for Hayden Abbott. Two things dictated this: Frank had made an outstanding appearance in the regionals, and his additional five inches in height would help against the number one rebounding team in the nation. The other forward, All-American Bob Boozer, and center, Jack Parr, would present an awesome front line. At guard spots would be DeWitz, who cut up Cincinnati with his seven points in the overtime, and Matuszak, who had played through and around legs under the basket for six lay-ups and 13 points against Oklahoma State.

Backing up that group would be Abbott, who was noted for his flair for the fast break; Holwerda, the good-shooting guard; and the stalwart all-around athlete, Fischer. These would be the first line reserves. The bench strength was another asset in the Wildcats' favor.

K-State would need all its capabilities in the first game, facing Seattle and their scoring ace, Elgin Baylor. Baylor was considered by many as good as Oscar Robertson. Tex made his team aware of the many tricks that Seattle used. One, for example, was their capitalizing on the opponent's fast break. Instead of every man rushing to defend, Seattle would have at least one player hang back, so that when a goal or rebound occurred the ball could be fired the length of the court for a quick, easy basket.

Sports Illustrated wrote prior to the game that each of the four teams had one man that could be considered the "bellwether" of the group – the player that could indicate which direction the game might go. For instance, Wilt Chamberlain often could spark the KU five to play brilliant basketball. So, too, Seattle had Elgin Baylor. With his sharp shooting, he might stir his team to play its best. The writer's opinion was that K-State's man to watch in that category was the center, Jack Parr. Parr's beautiful soft hook shots from as far out as 20 feet, along with his determined defense, could stymie the opponent. The unknown factor was Parr's moodiness. But if all went well, said the writer, K-State would be his pick to win the crown.

The night before the first game, however, Parr suffered an emotional "melt-down" and went into an uncontrollable rage. In the team doctor's room, his restraint broke down and he lost all focus. Tex was summoned. Parr physically attacked Tex with a choking hold. The doctor and coach managed to restrain Parr, who was penitent afterward and insisted that he could play ball. Tex didn't want to tighten the taut string on Jack's fragile emotions, but alongside this concern he had to consider the team's effectiveness and morale. He decided to play Jack intermittently, as needed.

The team knew nothing about what had happened, nor were they aware of similar events that had taken place during the season – outbursts that had been carefully dealt with and concealed. The team doctor had been counseling Jack, and those in the know felt they could deal with the problem privately.

For the team it therefore came as a shock on game night when Jack, sullen and silent, entered the locker room late. He slammed his locker and didn't speak to any of the squad. No one today seems quite certain, but it is thought that Jack did start the game and was pulled out at halftime. Tex summoned Glen Long to take up a forward position, switched Boozer to the post, and gave no explanation to the team for the sudden changes. The players went back on the court, dazed.

At home, those of us watching on television were stunned and disbelieving. This didn't look like our team. Where, we wondered, was their fighting spirit? Why were they looking so disjointed? In my sorority sister's small study room, a group of us sat speechless. Finally, someone uttered a very discouraging remark about the fact that maybe our team had been overrated. That was stinging to me and I tried to defend them, but was, in fact, thinking the same thing. They all looked as if they'd been caught with bright lights in their eyes, unable to function rationally.

NCAA FINALS
Vs. SEATTLE UNIVERSITY

The headlines afterward stated that Cinderella Seattle had crushed the favored Kansas State and that said it all. The Wildcats, in confusion, lost their composure to a fired up Seattle team. It was an almost unbelievable runaway victory in front of the 18,500 in attendance in Louisville. At one point, K-State went for nine and a half minutes without scoring a point. Elgin Baylor, Seattle's all-American, scored 23 points and snared 22 rebounds and was supported with his teammates' outstanding play. K-State never really even got in the game. At one point, Baylor even embarrassed one of our players defending him by bouncing the ball off his head.

Boozer and Frank tied for points scored, with 15 each. Matuszak put in seven, DeWitz had six, Glen Long and Jack Parr each had four. K-State shot only 32% from the field against Seattle's 46%. In rebounding K-State was simply overwhelmed, getting only 33 rebounds while Seattle pulled down 56. The final score was Seattle-73, K-State-51.

Tex was quoted following the game. "They came to play – and we didn't. We knew they were good and that Baylor is a great one. I don't know when we have played worse." Roy DeWitz, K-State's ace backcourt man, said, "We beat ourselves." Don Matuszak, the other guard, commented, "We had the opportunity, but we couldn't do anything with it." Several of the players grumbled, "We couldn't do anything right. They got ahead and made us look silly." Another said, "We simply had a hard time adjusting. If we'd only known what was going on…"

Seattle had fun toying with the Wildcats and making them look like they were just having a scrimmage. It had not been easy to watch.

Vs. TEMPLE UNIVERSITY

K-State's fortunes continued downward as they lost to Temple in the consolation game. Temple's win placed them third in the tourney and the Wildcats took fourth. Temple won in a come-from-behind surge to overtake the Cats.

K-State went ahead at the start of the game and began to look like they had all year. Parr started the game, but rested periodically, and Boozer would shift to the post position. The team kept adjusting and re-adjusting. Boozer, Frank, and Abbott put in most of the points in the first half, with Boozer hitting for ten, and Frank and Abbott for eight each. The Wildcats led at halftime 39-28.

In the second half, all-American Guy Rodgers and sophomore guard, Bill Kennedy, took command for the Owls. Kennedy had five field goals in the first ten minutes, taking feeds off Rodgers for layups down the middle. Rodgers scored 17 points himself for the game, while Kennedy had a total of 23 points.

The Cats shot 39% for the first half, but averaged only 28.3% for the game. The Owls hit only 25% in the first half, but came back in the 2nd half with deadly shots, pushing their game average to 35%. Rebounding was almost even with Temple snaring 54 and K-State grabbing 51. Boozer was high for the Cats with 12 rebounds, and Frank and Parr pulled in ten each.

The final score was 67-57. Boozer was high point man with 19 points, Abbott had 14, Frank got eight, Parr had seven, DeWitz six, and Matuszak three. The players were disappointed and upset, as was Tex. Some fans even laughed at the Wildcats and made fun of their efforts on the court. The Cats had been defeated by teams they had studied, teams everyone had predicted they could beat.

Even sportswriters called it a "humiliating" experience. What had happened, they asked, to the super Wildcat team? Where was their spirit, their will to win? The writers speculated. One thought the Wildcats were overpowered. Another suggested they didn't have the heart for the fight. Yet another believed they were not concentrating and had given Seattle and Temple the mental edge. Actually, all guesses were correct.

The Wildcats had come to play. This was a talented group, one that did not revolve around just one star. The effort was always a *group* effort. They didn't like to lose. The players knew Tex was a good coach, and Tex had said the team was an easy and fun group to coach. All of these young men would become college graduates. They were determined to be winners.

But an unexpected twist of fate put them in complete disarray. They were in shock and they were perplexed. Probably the team could have adjusted to the sudden and complete re-alignment of the cast, but there was no forewarning. They saw their teammate in dire trouble and didn't understand the complexities. It took their collective breath away. This had been a team fighting to win; it had become a bunch of individuals trying to understand, to cope – to try to continue playing without any knowledge of what was happening. The players' ability to concentrate seemed to disappear.

After the games, Roy and Jack played in All-Star games. Jack appeared to be okay, but once back in Manhattan he was admitted to the local hospital, then later transferred to another facility that was better equipped to handle his malady.

Everyone on campus was sympathetic, though they still remained in the dark as to what had occurred. Wildcat fans had been stunned and in disbelief at the team's performance in Kentucky, but the hearts of the entire campus and the town of Manhattan were big and understanding. Though details were not disclosed, the word was that something had snapped and Jack was in trouble. At the time, any subject involving a personal issue was not one to deal with publicly.

Societal restrictions of that time determined what we did and did not discuss. Some topics were best left unscrutinized. We didn't inquire about certain things with the vets who returned from war; we didn't ask personal questions; we didn't stir up any kind of troublesome issue. Alcoholism, prejudices, homosexuality, emotional problems, grief, unmarried mothers, adultery, sex before marriage, even sex *after* marriage – a whole slew of topics were kept hidden from view. Historians have designated that period of the fifties as the "quiet" culture, a time for everything and everybody to be *happy*. The war period was over and we were *happy* that so many had come home. We saw only *happy* TV shows like "Father Knows

Best" and "Ozzie and Harriet." We heard only *happy* lyrics on our radios and TVs. We kept our troubles beneath the surface.

The K-State Wildcats – the team that had been slated to take the big prize – ended up 3rd in the AP poll, 4th in the UPI poll. Then and in the years to come, that 1958 NCAA tournament would be talked about very little.

All of the seniors, to a man, went on to graduate. The sophomores and juniors would return, and they too would obtain their four-year diplomas.

At the end-of-season basketball banquet and presentation awards, **Bob Boozer was honored for his selection to the consensus All-American first team.*** Bob had proved that he could do it all: rebound, shoot, play defense, and perform as a team player. He had been outstanding in all areas, and his easy personality made him a favorite on campus. **Roy DeWitz and Jack Parr both received All-American honors** and both were drafted by the pros: Roy in the third round by Detroit and Jack in the tenth round by Cincinnati. Both also played in All-Star games.

To add to the excitement the team had generated, **Coach Winter was named NCAA Coach of the Year.** He was the youngest Division I coach ever to receive that honor. The Manhattan Booster Club, in appreciation, presented him with a new car.

Teammates selected their outstanding guard **Roy DeWitz as their Honorary Captain**, and named **Don Matuszak as Most Inspirational Player**.

The All Big Seven team named by UPI that year consisted of these players: **

Bob Boozer, forward – Kansas State
Joe King, forward – Oklahoma
Wilt Chamberlain, center – Kansas
Roy DeWitz, guard – Kansas State
John Crawford, guard – Iowa State

**Big 12 (formerly Big Eight) record books show the 1957-58 All Big Seven Team as:
- **Bob Boozer, Kansas State**
- Ron Loneski, Kansas
- Wilt Chamberlain, Kansas
- **Jack Parr, Kansas State**
- John Crawford, Iowa State

Big Seven Player of the Year: Bob Boozer
Big Seven Coach of the Year: Tex Winter

*During those years, the consensus All-America players were selected from those who had received recognition from the following: Associated Press, United Press International, National Association of Basketball Coaches, International News Service, Newspaper Enterprises Association, and Look Magazine.

Others on the 1957-58 1st team All-America were Elgin Baylor (Seattle), Wilt Chamberlain (Kansas), Oscar Robertson (Cincinnati), Guy Rodgers (Temple), and Don Hennon (Pittsburgh).

The 2nd team All-America was made up of Pete Brennan (North Carolina), Archie Dees (Indiana), Dave Gambee (Oregon State), Mike Farmer (San Francisco), and Bailey Howell (Mississippi State).

***

The school year was coming to a close. The NCAA tourney was not forgotten, just placed in the past, as all events ultimately are. We stashed the memory of the season's ending in the 'unfortunate happening' category. We refused to let it diminish the year's heroics, or the pride the student body felt for the team and the school.

We students were busy: cramming for exams and planning the summer. As we packed suitcases and boxes for our trips home, we were still talking about the miracle team, the team that wouldn't quit, the team that upset Oscar Robertson and Cincinnati and went on to the Final Four.

Don and I had dated most of the year and it was hard to say our farewells. We had been a "couple" on campus, though we never went "steady." We kept our feelings disguised, but that was hard to do with the chemistry between us. Those feelings became almost frightening, for we did not want to make personal commitments due to other priorities. I was imagining a future for myself that looked limitless. Don was dedicated, for the immediate future, to the game of basketball.

1958-59: A PATCHED-TOGETHER TEAM

In Kansas the summer of 1958 happened as usual. Wheat was harvested in June, the heat rose into the 100s, and the farmers talked of rain – either too much or too little. Many K-State students spent the summer working in the fields, driving tractors or combines, or hauling the wheat in trucks. Quite a few students were employed in town or community businesses that did well economically in the harvest season. Harvest hands poured into our farming communities for weeks as the combine crews worked from south Texas all the way to the Dakotas following the crop harvest. The signal that autumn was just around the corner came with the intense heat of August.

Labor Day rang the bell for the students at Kansas State; school got off to an official start at the end of that week. Students moved into dorms, private rooms, sorority and fraternity houses, and began making up their schedules. Lines formed outside the registration hall as students signed up for classes and pulled their cards. By now, most of us were acquainted with the system; we even pulled cards for friends. No one envied the poor freshmen!

One big reunion – that's what September felt like. The campus still had fewer than 7,000 students, so the atmosphere was easy-going and fun-filled even though summer's heat still smothered us. Sororities and fraternities arrived a week early so they could conduct Rush Week and select new members. Then the little town came alive with a swarm of students. Manhattan merchants picked up the pace, rejoicing in the increased business and the joy of welcoming back the students.

Get-acquainted events were held, groups exchanged open house invitations, and students gathered in the Student Union. This was generally the best time of the year, for classes hadn't yet worked up to full steam.

The talk on campus soon rolled around to the inevitable: How would the basketball team perform this year? We were missing two honorable-mention All-American players: Roy DeWitz, the hustling guard; and Jack Parr, the big man in the center. There were three senior veterans – Don Matuszak, Jim Holwerda, and our All-American Bob Boozer – but bench strength was questionable. Some returning squad members were non-lettermen, and only four had seen action in at least half of last year's games. Could Tex fill the void and, if so, what kind of line-up would he have? It was one of our biggest pastimes: discussing, prognosticating, and evaluating the basketball team's prospects.

K-State had come a long way in the past few years and now had their first-ever 1st team All-American in Bob Boozer. He was talented, no doubt, but needed a good supportive cast to propel him on his path to greatness. Bob had been an outstanding high school player, but had not been highly recruited. Our rival, KU, had contacted him, but Bob didn't envision getting much playing time with a team that had Chamberlain, so he didn't pursue talks with them. Instead, he had driven to K-State and talked to Tex, but Tex had been a bit skeptical, for he had heard that Bob might have a problem with his temper. Tex left him sitting in the waiting room while he checked with Howie, an assistant coach. Howie had seen Bob play and said that he had talent. Bob still had to wait, though, for the athletic department's last scholarship had been offered and

Tex was waiting to hear if the player accepted. Eventually, Bob got that last scholarship.

Supporting Bob would be his roommate and good friend, Don Matuszak. Don had had only one year of high school experience, but his coach had seen potential and contacted Tex. The high school coach knew Tex – and knew that Tex treated his players fairly and taught them good fundamentals. He told Tex he thought this kid could play on the college level. Tex took the coach's word and offered Matuszak a scholarship to K-State. Tex had never seen Don play, he later recalled.

Jim Holwerda, from the nearby town of Lindsborg, was a high school standout that Tex had recruited when he saw his shooting accuracy. Jim had wanted to stay close to home because he had a serious girlfriend and his family and friends could easily make the trip to Manhattan. Jim was just the kind of player Tex looked for: nice, nice-looking, smart, and athletic. He would fit right in any lineup.

Also returning were veteran reserves who had contributed to last year's success: Bill Guthridge, a junior out of Parsons, Kansas, who had come to K-State at the urging of Tex. He had been a very good player in high school and then had played a year in a small junior college in his hometown. Bill took the opportunity to prove himself and started out with no scholarship. He later received one as he continued to contribute.

Then, there was Wally Frank, who had become a valuable member of the squad during the last season. Now a junior, this big, quiet guy with an easy grin was a terrific shooter and had the best shooting accuracy on the team in his sophomore year. He came from Norton, Kansas, in the western part of the state, and had largely been overlooked by colleges other than Wichita State and Kansas State.

Perhaps the most unusual cases of 'non-recruitment' were the two local boys who were now in their junior year – Sonny Ballard and Steve Douglas. Because it is highly unusual to find local small-town talent, especially in a Division I school, they were almost overlooked. They had played several sports together at Manhattan High and had always thought of themselves as future Wildcats. Sonny's father owned a sporting goods business in town, and Steve's father was a professor at the school. They had to use some influence to talk to Tex, who decided to take both, probably because of Steve's size and Sonny's all-around athletic ability. Both Sonny and Steve were academically oriented; Tex figured they could quickly learn his style of play. Steve later said he never talked to Tex at that early stage – his dad did the negotiating.

Also, there was Jerry Johnson, a junior from Hutchinson, Kansas, who had been an outstanding high school player and chose K-State because of its noted school of veterinary medicine.

In this beginning of the 1958-59 season, the players were wondering who was going to be around, for rumors had been circulating that there weren't enough players to fill the bench. Twelve players were required. Chances for another successful season didn't look too promising. In the end Tex did acquire enough players, though no one seems to recall exactly how that came to pass.

Some say there was an ad in the school's newspaper, *The Collegian,* asking for anyone who had played high school or junior college ball to come try-out. Others believe that Tex happened to think of a couple of students who had played elsewhere and personally invited them to practice with the team. At any rate, three players were added at the last minute: Gary Balding, from Hazelton, Kansas; Glen Hamilton, from Partridge, Kansas; and Mickey Heinz from Claflin, Kansas. The latter two had played at a state junior college; Balding had played a year at Oklahoma State and dropped out of school temporarily to work.

After the initial somewhat-relaxed week of fun activities, shopping for books and supplies, and finding classes, school moved into first gear. The month of September slipped by, the leaves turned to fall colors, and football season turned into basketball season. Interest in the new basketball players intensified. All bets were on who would be the starters. Tex himself did not know. He always said the right combination of personalities, attitudes, and skills were necessary to make a team of five players, and he was beginning that search. This was his sixth year as head coach and he had brought national attention to the school and the small town of Manhattan. The fans were full of anticipation: Could he repeat his success this year?

At this time a tall slender nice-looking football player from Texas joined the team. Cedric Price became the second black on the team. He had looked promising as a freshman and there was hope that he would prove to be just the right ingredient for the "magic mix." Cedric had proven himself on the football field, especially as a pass receiver. Tex liked the fact that Cedric had muscular strength but could also run.

As the 1958-59 pre-season practice got underway, it was anybody's guess as to how this team would fare without Parr and DeWitz. Years later, the players all said that from the first days of practice they were optimistic that this could be another fantastic year. The returned players had close friendships, so they could almost read one another's minds, and their roles seemed defined. The players' respect for each other and the coaching staff was strong.

As adults looking back, those who played that year commented that they felt the group had all the right ingredients, patched together as they seemed to be. They had height, depth, desire to succeed, a sense of togetherness, a lack of jealousy, and confidence in their ability as a team. Most firmly believed they would see an even greater season than the one before – quite a lot of optimism from such a diverse group!

Boozer and Matuszak had thoroughly enjoyed rooming together their junior year and requested to do so again their senior year. Their preference of one of the "turret" rooms on the corners of the old field house was granted and, as before, they had a third roommate in the small room. Don and Bob's friendship was evident, both on and off the court. They simply *liked* each other and nothing that either of them ever said or did changed that fact. They shared stories of their lives, commiserated over everyday problems, talked about the future, and discussed whatever was on their minds.

On the court they supported each other, but with no preference over anyone else on the team. It was a unique bond in many ways: Matuszak came from Cicero, Illinois, a town noted for its stance against black citizenry, and Boozer came from an environment where his friends were generally from the black community. Though civil rights were not always recognized in the community, the difference in their races was never an issue for these two teammates and roommates. Occasionally in the evenings or after a game they would go downtown to get a snack. There was a place or two that wouldn't serve Boozer. One establishment welcomed him during the season, but put his food into a paper bag for carry out when the season was over. When anything like that occurred, without a word between them or with the clerk, Don and Bob simply walked out.

The Big Eight coaches, in their pre-season prognostication, believed the Wildcats would be the top team to beat. There were, however, voiced reservations. Some coaches expected that Oklahoma and Iowa State would be tough competitors. They also said that in their opinion, if the Wildcats won the conference they wouldn't win as many games as they had in the previous year. Oklahoma State would be playing in the conference for the first time. Kansas had lost Wilt Chamberlain to the Harlem Globetrotters. Some general assessments by sportswriters at the time:

- Nebraska will be one of the most entertaining teams, with their two aces, Hershell Turner and Al Maxey. They might be as tough as any team in the conference. They like to pull surprise plays, and have fun playing.
- Oklahoma is ready to threaten with Bob Stoerner, 6'8", Jack Marsh, 6'7", and Del Heide, 6'6 1/2". Guards Denny Price and Buddy Hudson might be good. They like to play aggressively and foul quite a bit.
- Missouri is having a hard time, although they have talented individuals. They probably won't be a top contender.
- Oklahoma State has 6'8" center Arlen Clark, but little to support him. They probably will not be as strong as usual.
- Iowa State has a good coach (Bill Strannigan), and they are tough at the guard spots, but are looking for sophomore, 6'7" Henry Whitney, and 6'4" Ted Ecker, to start looking better. At center 6'7" John Krocheski is their best hook shooter and a great all-around player.
- Colorado could be the biggest surprise of the conference. They have the best shooting team. Gerry Schroeder at 6'1" and Don Walker, 6'6", are two of the finest and most experienced players in the conference. They are predicted to be in the race all the way.
- Kansas should not be counted out. Ron Loneski at 6'5" and 217 lbs. has been one of the best players in the conference the past two years. Also, 6'6" Bill Bridges was the top rebounder in the conference. Their backcourt players will be tough.

- Kansas State will take some going to keep up the pace and everyone will be gunning for them. Tex has the coaching know-how to pull it off - with Don and Bob representing the most exciting (and dangerous) players, and the supporting cast of Wally Frank, Steve Douglas, and Sonny Ballard. Boozer is the top scorer in the conference. Cedric Price, a 6'6" sophomore and football player is coming along fast. Front line reserves are Jim Holwerda, Bill Guthridge, Mickey Heinz, and Gary Balding.

Tex Winter was not so optimistic. He always maintained, "A basketball game can turn on a trifle." One or two close games could throw off all predictions. Tex expressed concern over the loss of Parr and DeWitz. They had both been top defensive players. On the positive side he did have three starters back: Boozer and Frank, both 6'8", and guard Don Matuszak, listed as 6'0" though only 5'11". Questions swirled in the coach's mind as to how best to use his big men and who to play outside with Matuszak. Tex commented to the press: "I feel we could be a better team this year, but I seriously doubt if we can match last year's record for two reasons. First, last year's schedule was very hard, but this year's is even tougher and, secondly, there's no question but what everything went our way last year – that is, we had no crippling injuries. We can't count on that again." He cited his biggest concerns – mainly that the team lacked depth. "We have fewer basketball players than we've had in the last three years."

Just as the school year started, I competed in a contest in California – my longest trip from home, my first airplane ride, and an eye-opening experience. I spent a week seeing the sights of Los Angeles and San Francisco, meeting girls from other parts of the country, living in a luxurious home, and encountering situations never before imagined. The finale was a parade in downtown Berkeley, home of the University of California, where we were all introduced as we drove through the main part of the city. Having won the contest, I rode on a float while the other girls were in individual convertibles. "Why," I remember asking, "were some of the girls flanked by security while others of us weren't?" The answer stunned me: It was needed protection for the ones from certain areas of the South, where civil rights were a contentious issue. That was hard for me to fully understand. My world was so comfortable, so protected. Having had only limited access to TV and more interest in campus events and my studies than current events, I had been unaware.

Two weeks before the season opener, Bob Boozer was voted "Favorite Man on Campus." It was then, I believe, that the reality hit me. This might have been headline news on other campuses or in other states, but not at our school. Now, attuned to the national news more than ever, I knew that some of the schools in the South wouldn't even participate in integrated NCAA events. But that certainly was not the case at Kansas State. Boozer was the natural choice; he was friendly, outgoing, and an outstanding athlete.

Two weeks later Bob became the favorite man on the basketball court when he put in 45 points to give K-State a decided victory over Purdue in the season opener. He broke two K-State and field house records with that tally and his 23 free throws. (Both previous records were set by Dick Knostman, against Oklahoma, in 1953.)

Winter had high praise for the Purdue team. "It's too bad they had to lose their first game, especially since it was kind of humiliating. Actually, they have one of the top teams in the country." Going into the game, Boozer was fending off reports that he planned to go pro. The word had somehow circulated that he was going to join the Harlem Globetrotters, as Wilt Chamberlain had done the year before. Boozer denied even having any contact with them, saying, "I'm definitely interested in playing basketball the rest of the season for Kansas State and Coach Tex Winter. And

I'd like to finish my college education before even thinking about playing pro ball."

The schedule did seem tougher, as Tex had predicted. The second game of the season was with Indiana, winner of the previous year's Big 10. Howie Shannon, who usually did the scouting, pointed out that he had seen Indiana play for the last five or six years and "they impressed me more this year than at any time in the past." He added that they had a lot of basketball talent even at this early stage of the season.

Howie and Tex had been correct in their assessments, as Indiana gave the Wildcats a hard-fought game that eventually went into overtime. With 12,000 fans watching in disbelief, the Cats blew a 16-point lead. With 2:41 left in the game they trailed by five points. The regulation game ended on a highly disputed call as K-State's Cedric Price and Indiana's Frank Radovich both went up for a rebound with only 19 seconds on the clock. The Big 10 official called it a jump ball; the Big Eight official called it a foul. The difference was probably from the viewing point, but Price was fouled. He missed the first, but hit the second, tying the score and sending it into overtime. K-State prevailed: 82-79.

An obvious esprit de corps was growing among this group of players. Tex was the teacher, the players his students, and the respect and affection were mutual. No player can remember being admonished during a game or having an unpleasant encounter with any of the coaches. When Tex had anything to say, it was usually in general terms. He showed mistakes on film. If someone had missed a pass, he'd say, "Be alert." If, when rebounding, a player were out of position, Tex would simply remark about position and effort.

The season was going well both for the team and for the relationship between Don and me. We were still cautious about voicing our feelings openly and certainly didn't show them. Our greetings on the campus or in the Union were pleasant, but not much different from the way we greeted other friends. There was always a trepidation hovering over us. We couldn't become serious. Not now, maybe never. We had so much fun together, but we were from entirely different backgrounds, different religions – and had very different plans for the future.

The players were enjoying themselves, laughing and joking at every opportunity. During game films they would sarcastically tease each other, calling out "Great pass!" when someone goofed, or "Nice shot" if a player's attempt went erratic. No one was exempt from their humor, not even the coaches – or the trainer, "Porky" Morgan, who was himself a jokester. The guys especially enjoyed teasing assistant coach Howie Shannon, who was laid back and had a deadpan wit. They would tell him that his scouting report sounded just like what they'd read in the sports section of the paper. Bill Guthridge remembers an incident when Howie gave a scouting report on Walt Bellamy, an outstanding player from Indiana. Before the game Howie stated that Bellamy "has no left hand," meaning, supposedly, that he was a right-hand shooter only. During their game Bellamy lobbed in 16 points from all areas of the floor, using either hand equally well. A few days later Matuszak found a glove on the floor and yelled at Howie, "Look! It's Bellamy's left hand!"

After one out-of-town game, two of the guys wanted to slip out of the hotel to meet a friend who had come a long way to see the game. They knew that Howie would make his nightly room check, so they used blankets to make up their beds to look like they were in the beds, and sneaked out the back door for a quick beer. As soon as the door closed behind them they heard a startling click and realized they were locked out. Focused then on simply getting back inside, they forgot the beer and went to the front of the hotel and peered inside. They saw only one man sitting in the lobby reading the paper, so they quietly walked in. As they did, the man's newspaper slowly descended and Howie said, "Hello, boys." And that was the end of the story: Howie never said another word about it.

Boozer and Matuszak began a ritual that continued through all the home games. Before each game the cheerleaders put up a giant hoop covered with paper and decorated with a Wildcat figure. In the locker room, the team sat on benches facing Tex as he gave his "chalk talk" with final instructions. Don and Bob both positioned themselves on the ends of the benches, closest to the exit. They planted their feet and continued to edge closer to the end, like racehorses at the starting gate. When Tex gave the "go" Boozer and Matuszak made it a contest to see who could get through the doors and up the steps and be the first to leap through the hoop. Their ritual became a reliable entertainment in the locker room, and the fans loved seeing the team members break through the paper with grins and enthusiasm.

Tex tolerated all this and probably enjoyed it, but remained firm in his role as teacher. He saw that the joking and fun were making the players bond tightly – making them care about the team's efforts above any individual effort. He knew they were able to focus when it was time and that their vision was always to win. The players remember Tex's admission that he couldn't give them the incentive to win or a pep talk to get them ready to play. He made it clear that his job was to teach them the fundamentals, and their task was to mentally prepare themselves. Several times he simply skipped the talks and said, "Go out and have fun!"

This non-conference schedule was going to get even harder. After defeating two Big 10 teams, one a squeaker, the squad now prepared for a "Western swing," as they referred to it. They were on the road to play three outstanding teams in four days: University of California and San Francisco University on succeeding days, then Brigham Young only two days later. Cal appeared to be the toughest to beat; they had just won three straight games, including wins over San Francisco and St. Mary's. All of the coastal teams were highly touted.

The Cats were ranked nationally at #2 by UPI and #3 by the AP, but they were facing high-caliber opponents. With their West Coast agenda, they were putting their ranking on the line.

The team left without Glen Long, who had injured his knee in the Indiana game. Tex had hoped that Glen would be the key to rounding out the team, but he saw no reason to take any chances with the knee. Besides his talent, the team would miss Glen's humor. He and Matuszak provided much of the jocularity that eased tenseness and relieved dull moments. K-State would probably replace injured Long with Steve Douglas, their 6'4" junior.

Tex worried about the Cats' ability to handle the ball against the press. He felt the team was inexperienced in that aspect. He also continued to express concern about the lack of depth, for the hastily assembled group of reserves had not yet seen much actual playing time. He could see that the players were enjoying playing the game and playing together. Their determination as a team proved a driving force in each game.

Their first opponent, University of California, was 12-3 in their conference play the previous year, 19-9 overall, and had tied Oregon State for the Pacific Coast title. Coach Pete Newell was playing with only five lettermen back, but one of those was Daryl Imhoff, a great 6'10" center. San Francisco, NCAA champions in 1955 and '56 and NCAA regional champions last year, had lost every starter from the previous squad but was still considered tough on defense. This year, so far, they were still floundering and had a 1-4 record.

The Wildcats barely defeated the California Bears in a down-to-the-wire game that gave the Cats their third victory in a row and ruined Cal's record three-game winning streak. An All-American performance by Bob Boozer left even the partisan crowd impressed. Following the 68-65 victory, appreciative fans swamped Boozer, asking for his autograph.

Sportswriters say that the ability to win the close ones is the mark of a winner. The victory over California was close, but a 53-52 win over San Francisco the following night proved to doubters that the Wildcats could come through in the clutch. Coach Winter remarked, "We're playing under pressure. Our opponents are going to play their best ball against us. It means a lot to their prestige to knock us off."

His next words proved prophetic. "It's getting to be too much of a life or death matter. We're playing every game like it was for the national title. I'm concerned about it. With the schedule we've got, we *have* to play that way to win. But you can't expect to play that way every game and keep a sharp edge. It wouldn't hurt if we lost a couple. I don't want to, but it wouldn't hurt. It might be the making of our team."

The contest with BYU was only two days later and the Cougars were ready for the Wildcats. Boozer was not in top-notch form: he had split his tongue in the San Francisco game, and was hampered by a knee injury in the second half. Excuses aside, BYU took them by surprise as the Wildcats ran out of gas and Boozer was held to only eight points for the game. The final score was BYU-77, K-State-68.

The Wildcats had no time to lick their wounds because on their return they were to play the big double-header Sunflower Classic again, and as before they would alternate with Kansas University against top-ranked teams on both courts. In just four days, K-State would be matched against both St. Joseph and North Carolina State on successive nights. They needed to focus on those very tough teams.

Cincinnati, Kentucky, and Kansas State now held positions 1-2-3 in the second Associated Press balloting. But the contest for first place was even closer than the first poll. The Cincinnati Bearcats, who had maintained a 96-point margin scoring average during their first three games in the season, edged out Kentucky by just one first-place vote. They had 938 points in the balloting, followed by Kentucky with 920 points, and Kansas State with 741. In fourth place was North Carolina State, then Tennessee, Northwestern, West Virginia, Mississippi State, Xavier, and North Carolina in tenth place.

SUNFLOWER CLASSIC (12/19/58)
KU vs. ST. JOSEPH
&
K-STATE vs. NORTH CAROLINA STATE

In two heart-stopping games played in Manhattan with four nationally outstanding teams, there was no lack of suspense, talent, outstanding plays, or surprises. It was, and continues to be, one of the great moments in Ahearn Fieldhouse history. In the opening game, the St. Joseph Hawks showed some razzle-dazzle in an over-time win against the Chamberlain-less KU Jayhawks. The final score was 67-65 as the Jayhawks came up short on shooting percentages. The crowd had just begun to get their pulse rate down when the Wildcats faced off in the following game against the great North Carolina State team, which was touted for its overall ability and especially noted for its all-America candidate, Lou Pucillo. He headed this fourth-ranked team.

Pre-publicity centered not only on the match-ups of four nationally ranked teams, but also the duel between two of basketball's best "little men." Tex Winter called Don Matuszak, his 5'11" guard "maybe the best little man in basketball in the nation," and said that Don always keyed the Wildcat floor game with his exceptional ball-handling and playmaking. Don had huge hands and could easily move the ball from one hand to another. At that time "palming the ball" or rolling it over while dribbling was consistently called a violation, so it was, again, another limitation of the game.

North Carolina State featured 5'9" Lou Pucillo. Coach Everett Case called him "one of the greatest basketball players I've ever seen, much less coached" in forty years of coaching. Both young men were outstanding at passing and dribbling; their match-up would be an exciting contest.

The game opened with the Wildcats missing their first nine shots, but they almost caught up by the half, trailing only 36-33. With Matuszak and Frank pacing the Cats, the score was finally tied at 44 and from that point on, it was neck and neck with the lead never more than three points for either team. NC State was leading 63-60 when Matuszak put the heat on and stole the ball three times in the final three minutes. The Cats were up 66-63 when Pucillo shot one of his long and exciting jump shots, making it 66-65. Ballard came through with a layup to put the score at 68-65; then, with only 28 seconds on the clock, NC State's DeStefano grabbed a rebound and made a twisting layup to cut the lead to 68-67. With just 18 seconds left, Matuszak was fouled and hit one for the final score of 69-67. Pucillo took one more shot, but missed, and Boozer grabbed the rebound.

The game plan for North Carolina State had been to rein in Boozer near the basket, leaving the Wildcat guards open. When Jim Holwerda, the go-to man for outside shooting, was not hitting his mark, Tex sent in Ballard, who became as hot as his red hair. He shot five long ones, grabbed the ball out of a pile of big men under the basket, and banked in a layup in the final seconds.

The game was a test of teamwork for K-State. Sonny Ballard's surprise plays, Cedric Price's great work at the post, Don Matuszak's outstanding all-around play, Boozer's superb defensive work, and Wally Frank's cool steadiness made this a game to remember. When Boozer was in foul trouble with 14 minutes remaining on the clock, Price was sent in to relieve him. Price put in six crucial points as well as grabbing four rebounds and ball-hawking on defense.

Matuszak, however, was the man who spelled the difference. In a 1-3-1 defense, used after Boozer got in foul trouble, Matuszak stole the ball time and time again, to outshine Pucillo. He stole seven passes in the second half alone to throw the Wolfpack off guard. Pucillo, though, did let everyone know he was more than just a guard. He did some fancy dribbling and was the top scorer of the game with 21 points.

The game was the first defeat for the NC State team. Both teams now exhibited a 5-1 record.

Both teams had lost their centers during the game. Boozer left early in the second half with four fouls and John Richter fouled out for NC State with 8:10 left in the game. He had scored 17 points. Boozer was able to finish the game playing cautiously during the final minutes and ended with 19 points. He led both teams with 16 rebounds.

Always steady and coming through when needed, Wally Frank got 13 points and 8 rebounds. Ballard added 14 points, Matuszak eight, Price six, Douglas five, and Holwerda four.

The local Manhattan newspaper columnist, Dick Fensler, reporting on the game, called the four teams "the ultimate in thrills and spectacular play. The play of Don Matuszak alone in the game was worth the price of admission, and when you throw in the play of Lou Pucillo, you had the best basketball bargain in the nation Friday night. Both boys are great in every sense of the word.

Pucillo has the edge in scoring ability, but Matuszak is second to none in floor play, and ably demonstrated that Friday night by playing rings around the Wolfpack." Fensler added, "Credit should also be given to Bob Boozer for his ability to go 18 minutes without fouling and still contribute vital points, rebounds, and great defense to the winning rally."

Fensler also praised the newcomers in the lineup, Sonny Ballard and Cedric Price. They "were the heroes. Coming off the bench as they did, and playing the best ball of the season, they were the difference in the outcome."

K-STATE vs. ST. JOSEPH (12/20/58)

The doubleheader moved to Lawrence on the next night and Kansas State faced the mighty team from St. Joseph's, the unbeaten Hawks. They had won over KU the previous night, so still had an unblemished record. This was a Philadelphia team, a city that prized its basketball traditions. Many outstanding players had come from the playgrounds and city leagues of Philly, including the feared Jayhawker Wilt Chamberlain who had gone on to play for the Globetrotters, and the two outstanding players recruited by North Carolina State, Lou Pucillo and John Richter.

Matuszak, again performing his floor show for the 7,500 fans, cracked the game open in the second half and allowed the Cats to pull away. He scored 12 points in the game, ten of those in the second half.

Ballard, in his first starting role, also had 12 points and played well on defense. Douglas had six points and was very aggressive on the boards, pulling down nine rebounds in the first half, and finishing the game as the leading rebounder with 14. Price, who started the second half, with Boozer moving to the forward position, also had a great game and brought down 12 rebounds during the last 20 minutes. Wally Frank, who sat out most of the second half after hitting only one of 13 from the field in the first half, returned to action late in the game and hit eight quick points, to finish with 11.

The Cats started out hitting only 24% in the first half, but led 31-30 at intermission. Matuszak put K-State ahead for good in the second half with a jump shot, making it 35-33. Boozer upped that to 37-33, and Matuszak added five points in one minute and the board read 42-34. Tex started putting everyone into the game when the Wildcats were ahead 51-39. With three minutes on the clock, the score stood 57-50 and Frank hit his hot streak, for a final score of 68-53.

This night belonged to the Wildcats, and for the first time since the season opened they enjoyed a fairly easy win. Boozer had one of his best nights of the season as he hit for 26 points and was the game's top scorer. But he had plenty of help from Matuszak, Ballard, Douglas, Frank, and Price. It was a particularly poignant night because Manhattan fans saw two of their high school heroes take their place in the starting lineup – Sonny Ballard and Steve Douglas. It's doubtful that many, if any at all, Division I schools ever had that happen.

About this time Coach Winter took yet another unusual step: he invited Joe Vader from the football team to come join the basketball squad. He knew Joe was athletic, muscular, smart, and could be an asset. Joe said that he realized Tex was looking for a "banger"– someone to rebound in scrimmage against the taller guys – but he was excited nonetheless. He joined the reserves shortly after the Thanksgiving holiday.

While the Cats were catching fire, the relationship between Don and me was slowly losing its flame. So many factors were involved and we were too close to the situation to realize what was happening. In hindsight, I guess we knew that there were too many stumbling blocks and there was no reason to continue seeing each other. There was no denying the feelings between us, but it seemed pointless. We slowly drifted apart.

HOLIDAY TOURNAMENT (12/26-12/30, 1958)

This year would be my last chance to attend the now-Big Eight tournament in Kansas City. The event had become the great social mixer of the season. The fans put rivalry aside, and students from all schools came together for several days of fun and spirited cheering. I wanted to be part of this rite of the collegiate scene, and certainly wanted to root for our team – a team I had been following with great interest. A sorority sister's mother volunteered her apartment. A group of us could sleep on the floor. It was a memorable time! One night, students from several schools pitched in a dollar or two and rented a big meeting room at a hotel where everyone was welcome, no matter what their affiliation.

Coming into the tournament as favorites and now nationally ranked fourth in the nation, K-State was the team to beat. The Cats were in a fight to maintain their ranking, which changed every week. K-State and KU were in different brackets this year. K-State opened against Missouri, and in the same bracket, Oklahoma would face Iowa State. Kansas played their first game against highly regarded Colorado, while Oklahoma State, taking its place among the Big Eight for the first time, faced off against Nebraska.

Some thought the tough competition would be Oklahoma with its tall front line, and Colorado with its shooting ace, Gerry Schroeder. Most believed this tournament would show the depth of talent in the Big Eight overall, and that it would be a scramble to win the conference. K-State's first game, against Missouri, was not predicted to be a difficult victory, but then again, in this tournament anything could happen.

K-State had been re-grouping and experimenting with its strong bench talent. Coach Winter discovered an asset: Cedric Price was able to come into a game and take over as either a forward or a center. In the double-header, both Cedric Price and Sonny Ballard showed their talent, and Ballard – with two great performances – seemed to have won his way into the starting line-up. Price had been quite adept at sweeping for rebounds and substituting for anyone at any time. It was thought that he would probably be a regular sixth man, as Wally Frank had been last year. Another bright spot was the possible return of Glen Long, giving the Wildcats additional bench strength. Jim Holwerda, known for his ability to enter a game and get the needed outside shots, also added to the reserve power.

FIRST GAME OF TOURNAMENT
Vs. MISSOURI UNIVERSITY

In this first game, K-State was favored to take Missouri by 11 points. With Wally Frank and Bob Boozer taking command of the scoring, they were off and going in the first half, posting a 30-21 lead at intermission. The second half saw a different Missouri team, full of determination, and the Cats again had to fight to the finish to come up with the victory. This had become almost commonplace. Both Boozer and Ballard fouled out, but before leaving and with six minutes left in the game, Bob had taken a new Kansas State scoring record with 1,190 points, beating Jack Parr's 1,184 points set during the last three years. When the game was over, the scoreboard read 69-66, with K-State on top.

The starters for the game were Boozer at center, Douglas and Frank at forward, and Matuszak and Ballard at guard positions. Frank led the scoring with 23 points; Boozer had 22, Price ten, Matuszak nine, Ballard four, and Douglas one.

Tex pointed out that his team missed the services of Jim Holwerda, a regular backcourt man, who had the flu. He further said, "This is going to be a rugged test for all the teams. We will have to play up to our top capability at all times if we're going to win the tournament. The same goes for the other teams, too."

Following the game, Coach Winter expressed his feelings. "Everybody thinks we're a lot better than the other clubs, but we're not. We're going to have to start shooting a lot better if we're going to live up to our reputation." In actuality, the Cats did outshoot Missouri percentage-wise, but Winter still wasn't satisfied.

"It's always nice to win 'em," he said. "And as long as we can keep winning and not shoot any better, I guess we're all right." The Missouri Tigers had played their usual aggressive and rugged game, and Winter said of them, "Their style of play is difficult to play against. It doesn't allow you the freedom you normally have." He was impressed with Missouri and considered them the dark horse of the conference.

Winter singled out Cedric Price for his outstanding effort on the boards. He pointed out the failure of the Cats to adjust quickly when Missouri switched from a zone to a man-to-man defense in the second half. Sportscasters congratulated Boozer on his record-setting performance, but he replied, "How many did Wally have? He sure pulled us out of that one!"

In the same bracket, Oklahoma won a hard-fought victory over Iowa State. The final score was 68-65.

2nd GAME OF TOURNAMENT
Vs. OKLAHOMA

Oklahoma coach Doyle Parrack was optimistic after the Kansas State-Missouri game. He felt that if the Wildcats played the same kind of ball against his team, then his team had a chance at winning. "I don't know how Tex felt about it, but I was surprised they didn't play any better than they did. We're going to have rebounding trouble against them, and we'll have trouble with Boozer, Frank, Matuszak…" – and his voice trailed off.

For the record, Coach Winter wasn't too disappointed, because he knew that Missouri was a difficult club to play against: they didn't let the other team relax for a minute. Winter was also upbeat about the effort of sophomore Cedric Price. "As the season progresses we'll probably use Price more at the pivot and let Boozer go back to the forward position," he said. Winter said of the Oklahoma team, "That is a fine team with plenty of size and I have said all along that they are going to be one of the top contenders in the league. Nothing I saw against Iowa State makes me alter that prediction."

It was true that the Wildcats had something to worry about. They had not been hitting a good percentage of their shots for the past five games. They had, however, won four of those games, mainly on the great rebounding of the three big men – Boozer, Price, and Frank. They also had a great defense that had often regained possession of the ball without permitting an opponent to shoot.

The starting line-up for the Oklahoma game would be Boozer at center, with Frank and Douglas at forward positions, and Ballard and Matuszak as guards. Jim Holwerda had recovered from his virus and would be back in action.

Oklahoma's line-up would be the biggest in the conference. They included Del Heidebrecht and Jack March, both 6'6" as forwards; Bill Stoermer, the 6'8" center; and guards Denny Price at 6'1" and Buddy Hudson at 6'2". Both guards were outstanding shooters from a distance.

Other teams making the semi-finals were Colorado, who sank Kansas 63-52, and Nebraska, who had dropped Oklahoma State

55-48. Neither team had been given much consideration going into the tourney. The conference was tough this year, though, and as many had predicted, anyone could be the champion.

The Wildcats were on the defensive attack against the Sooners from the start, and even though the Cats weren't shooting much early in the game, Oklahoma was generally not able to score because the K-State team was all over the court: stealing the ball, forcing Sooner errors, and creating havoc with the Oklahoma defense. In the first six minutes, the Wildcats hit only one field goal, but outscored the Sooners 17-15 as they hit 15 of 19 from the charity line.

Boozer hit 16 free throws in a row, setting a single-game record. (His total was 76 in tournament play, also a record.) The Cats hit 41 of their 50 free throws, while the Sooners made 17 of 25. Oklahoma had 21 field goals to K-State's 16. However, K-State was the victor with a final score of 73-59.

Boozer was the game's top scorer with 28 points. Wally Frank hit 19, Douglas had 10, Matuszak eight, Ballard four, and Holwerda and Price each had two. Oklahoma had four players leave the game on fouls, but K-State didn't lose a single one.

Shooting was not as good as Coach Winter had hoped it would be. He said, "We are tipping that ball a lot, keeping it alive on the offensive backboard, and that hurt our percentage. As for Boozer, it is something he will have to work on. He is worried about his scoring average and is simply pressing too hard. That scoring average is something he has to learn to cope with, as the pressure will be on him all season."

TOURNAMENT FINAL
Vs. COLORADO

The Kansas State-Colorado game proved to be a nail-biter. K-State was behind as much as nine points in the second half. But,

Boozer hit a tip shot, and Price put one in on a feed from Boozer then hit a free throw when he was fouled on the play. Price hit two more free throws to close the gap to 61-59. Wally Frank and Steve Douglas were adept at providing a screen for the big man who needed their help. Boozer later said that the Colorado pivot man, Don Walker, was "surprisingly tough."

Boozer made the winning basket with a deep hook shot when the clock read 2:01 to go in the game. With 27 seconds on the clock, Gerry Schroeder, Colorado's outstanding shooting forward who was being closely guarded by Steve Douglas, tried and missed a shot and Matuszak iced the victory by picking up the rebound. It was a hard-fought come-from-behind victory, but Kansas State edged out Colorado by a final score of 67-66, taking the tournament title.

Schroeder was high point man for Colorado, with 28 points. Boozer led all scoring with 32 points. That made Bob's total for the tournament 82 points. In his three tournaments – as a sophomore, junior, and now a senior, he had scored 214 points. The total was not enough, however, to surpass the three-year record of 222 points held by Clyde Lovellette, a former Jayhawker. Other scorers for K-State were Ballard with 12, Matuszak with ten, Frank nine, and Price four.

The sports headlines in the Kansas City paper the next morning announced in bold letters that the tournament title had been miraculously won by Kansas State. Below the headline was a quote from a sportswriter: "How did K-State manage to win? As their opponents have learned, this Wildcat team will not crack, continues to battle back, and will win, somehow, in the end."

Colorado coach Sox Walseth praised the effort of his team, saying that he "couldn't have asked for anything better. We should have won it."

Kansas State's pre-season tournament title was the first in the six years under coach Tex Winter. The team was ranked #3 nationally going into the tournament, but that same night #2 Cincinnati was defeated by North Carolina State in the Dixie Basketball Classic; and Michigan State, ranked #7, upset #4-ranked North Carolina by 17 points.

Named to the All-Tournament team were both Boozer and Matuszak from K-State, along with Schroeder from Colorado and Turner from Nebraska. Oklahoma State's Clark and KU's Loneski tied for 5th place.

***

Only a few days later we were all back in school, hitting the books and readying ourselves for the semester tests that were several weeks away. Our basketball players vigorously attacked their studies while also practicing in preparation for the first official conference game.

Opening the conference season on January 8th, the Cats traveled to Ames for their first game since the narrow victory over Colorado that had brought Coach Winter his first conference tournament final. If the tournament had pointed out one thing, it was that there existed only a small margin between the first and last teams. This promised to be a tough year for all eight teams. K-State, although still predicted to be the favorite, had won the final by only *one point*. The conference race would be exciting and unpredictable.

The match was another close, tense game, but K-State narrowly took the victory over Iowa State with a score of 59-56. Their coach, Bill Strannigan, was not unhappy about the outcome. He saw the positives in several of his players' performances. He felt that the Cats had as good a team as last year's when they finished fourth in the nation. He said, "K-State's got a good, sound, well-coached team. You know, many times those close games are won by coaching." He went on to state that it was a more evenly balanced conference than in years past and that any team could win any given game.

Speaking to the K-State Booster Club several days later, Coach Winter jokingly said about all the close wins, "I think it might be one of two things: we are just as good a team as our opponents and are winning on our superior coaching, or else we are such a superior team that we are winning in spite of the coaching!"

He continued: "Seriously, I hope the actual situation is somewhere between that. We are not head and shoulders above our opposition, as a lot of people seem to think we are… There are just too many fine basketball teams in the league, and in the nation, for anyone to dominate. One reason so many people think we are so much better than the rest in the Big Eight is because we are the only league team that is ranked nationally…Well, there are a lot of fine basketball teams in the nation that are not even ranked in the top 20, and all of them are capable of beating anyone else on a given night."

Winter agreed with Strannigan's assessment of the strength of the lead and the game that the Iowa State Cyclones had played. Winter did not so much think that his team had blown the wide lead as that Iowa State had simply surged back into the game.

Back home two days later, the Wildcats faced Colorado again, this time on their Manhattan court. In a stunning victory that proved Kansas State's many narrow victories were no fluke, they beat the Colorado Buffaloes in their easiest win so far in the season. With the final score 89-58, Tex Winter called it "one of our best efforts." Colorado's coach Sox Walseth seemed almost in shock as he said, "Kansas State tonight was as good as any team we have ever played against. They could have beaten anybody in the country tonight."

Tex attributed the win to the Cats' 1-2-2 zone defense – designed primarily to shut down Schroeder, the opponent's ace shooter – and to the Cats' overall hustle. He had good words for all the players, down to the last sub.

He had a special pat on the back for Don Matuszak. "You've got to give Matuszak a lot of credit, to get out of a sick bed and play with the spirit he did." Matuszak had been in the campus hospital until two hours before game time with an infected throat. He had run a temperature all the day before. When his fever went down Saturday he was given permission to play, provided he would return to the hospital immediately following the game. "I should play when I'm sick more often," cracked Matuszak. He said he felt a little weak, but otherwise felt no ill effects from playing, nor from running through and around the Buffaloes with his ball-handling antics.

Tex Winter was very happy with his reserves, explaining that this was the first time he'd had the opportunity to see some of them in action. He cited Steve Douglas as playing his best game. He said Sonny Ballard had "loosened up and played real well," and that Cedric Price "is coming along in good shape, particularly on defense and rebounding, and Boozer's shooting was terrific."

Two days after trouncing Colorado, K-State faced one of the biggest and strongest teams in the conference, Oklahoma University; but the Cats had been working more and more as a team in each game, and were ranked #3 nationally. They had no trouble with Oklahoma, posting a final score of 90-45!

Winter commented on the superb play from the bench. "We've got more depth this year than we had at the same time last year. We've got a real fine second five – in fact, a real fine third five, too!"

Referring to Cedric Price as his "sixth regular" now, Winter allowed that, "We've reached a point of playing the way we should be playing. We're hustling hard and have got the opponents playing our kind of game."

Sooner coach Doyle Parrack commented, "K-State played a great ball game. I thought this was a better ball club than the one that beat us last year. It's as good looking a team as I've seen. We were out-shot, out-defensed, out-hustled, and out-ball-handled tonight. I believe it's the worst beating I've ever had – and that's the story."

But that wasn't the *real* story. Either everyone forgot or everyone failed to mention that this was not a team of big names or highly recruited players. This was a hodgepodge team, thrown together like a crazy quilt, made up of players like Boozer, Matuszak, Ballard, and Douglas who had to ask for a chance to play. Their coaches or fathers had come to Tex on their behalf, or – as in Boozer's case – they came themselves, hat in hand, looking for an opportunity. Some were players that had been largely overlooked, or accepted the only scholarship offered. Some didn't even have scholarships.

The group had been pieced together with walk-ons and football players, and they succeeded beyond all expectations. This unlikely assemblage went against the top teams and the top players in the country, and showed that they had the desire, the determination, and the heart to be a real *team*. No one was jealous; no one was special. They competed for each other and for their school. They didn't even consider defeat; they simply refused to lose.

After a five-day break to allow for upcoming semester finals, the Cats went back on the court for a game with Missouri University in Columbia on January 17th. This rivalry was usually contentious, with both teams prepared for lots of action and very partial fans on both sides. However, in an unusual display of good sportsman-like conduct, there were no court battles and no roughhousing, and the fans were well behaved.

Sparky Stalcup, Missouri's coach, had just been criticized in the local paper for his team's performance. Missouri was in last place in the Big Eight, despite having a roster of talent. In a gesture of goodwill, Tex marched down to the newspaper office and let his support for Stalcup be known. He told Sparky after the game, "You've got one of the three best teams in the league. All they need is a victory to show them they can still win. Once they get it you're going to be tough to beat." Their needed victory wasn't to be that night, however, as the Wildcats walloped them 75-60.

The Tigers played hard and with concentration, but the Cats were too much in the end. Boozer was the only player who seemed to play well offensively, though, and that worried Tex. He talked about the way the Tigers would drop behind then close the gap. "When they closed that gap it was usually due to our missing three or four good shots. I figured that we would hit again soon, and we did. Of course, if we had gone a long period without hitting, it could have gotten mighty tight." Don Matuszak stymied the Tiger guards with his pressure on them. He hawked the ball and made many interceptions with at least six being converted into quick field goals for the Wildcats.

Boozer threw in a total of 30 points, jamming in seven in a three-minute period at the end of the game. The other starters and the entire bench contributed heavily as the Wildcats took the win easily.

In the rest of the Big Eight, Kansas, who was tied with K-State, dropped its first game 45-38 to Oklahoma. Nebraska won over both Iowa State and Missouri to pull up to a tie for second with KU. The conference race promised to be down to the wire.

Among teams in the national rankings, most would take the next week off for exams. The top four teams – North Carolina State, Kentucky, North Carolina, and Kansas State – would be idle, creating opportunity for other contenders such as Auburn,

Cincinnati, Michigan State, St. John, and West Virginia. Auburn had the longest major winning streak – 22 games, but they had largely been overlooked in national polls.

With semester finals behind them, the Wildcats played their next home game nine days later against Iowa State. In an amazing performance, they again recorded a commanding win by defeating the Cyclones, 78-55, in front of a crowd estimated to be around 7,500 – that, despite a huge snowfall during the afternoon. The game also was played between semesters and on a Monday night. This was the sixth straight conference loss for Iowa State and Kansas State's fifth straight victory.

The game signaled the end of the first semester and K-State was hit hard with one very significant grade "fatality." Sonny Ballard, an electrical engineering major, was declared ineligible. Sonny was a local high school standout student-athlete and had never had grade trouble before. However, this year's schedule and level of competition was daunting and hometown people shook their heads in sympathy and dismay. Tex, speaking to the local Boosters' Club, told the crowd that everyone felt badly about it, but none worse than Sonny, himself. "He's learned that there is just so much a person can do," said Tex. The coach hated losing Sonny for another reason. He had noted the great feelings of friendship among these team members, and knew that each one of the players contributed to the whole. He commented, "They have enjoyed playing more this year than last and seem to have greater incentive." Sonny would later say that the incident had been the greatest learning experience of his life.

Next on the schedule was a non-conference game at home for the Wildcats against one of their former greats, Jim Iverson, who was now coaching South Dakota State. Iverson had himself been coached by Tex Winter, and was the highest scoring guard in K-State history, with 309 points as a senior. That night Iverson watched his former coach's team beat his small college team by a score of 91-65.

Nebraska drew a capacity crowd in Lincoln's Coliseum when K-State made them their next and 12th straight victim on February 2nd. It wasn't a run-away, but the Cats finished the Huskers off with a final score of 50-43.

K-State was #3 now in the national poll, behind Kentucky and North Carolina, but Cincinnati had replaced North Carolina State as #4. This was the UPI poll, conducted by 35 leading coaches. They gave Kentucky 16 first place votes for a total of 316 points. North Carolina had nine first place votes and 294 points. K-State also received nine first place votes and 262 points. Cincinnati had 223 points, while North Carolina State tallied 217 points.

The Wildcats traveled to Boulder only five days later to face the Colorado Buffaloes. In a frantic, hotly contested duel, before a packed sold-out crowd of 7,000, the Wildcats finally gained the victory with a score of 70-59. That may have looked like an easy win, but it definitely was not. Colorado was tenacious to the end and, although down by 10 points with 7 minutes on the clock, they were still in pursuit.

The win gave the Wildcats a 2-game lead in the quest for the conference title. They remained unbeaten in the conference with their record of 7-0. Every other team had now lost at least twice. The Cats' overall record stood at 17-1.

The K-State Wildcats' victory over Colorado had been their 13th straight, matching the all-time school winning streak set by the 1950-51 team, which finished 2nd in the NCAA tournament and were named #3 and #4 by AP and UPI in the final polls. K-State now led the Big 8 with a 7-0 record and their match-up with Kansas University on Feb.11th would not only gain them another victory mark, but also help even out the win-loss records of the dueling teams. Local odds-makers thought K-State to be about a ten-point favorite, but nothing was predictable when these two state rivals met on the court. It had been especially disconcerting that the last six times the KU teams had come to Ahearn Fieldhouse they had gone home with the win.

This night, however, the Cats were determined and it took all the shooting, all the playmaking, and all the coaching to pull out the win, but the score stood at 82-72 at the buzzer. The victory boosted Kansas State to an overall record of 18-1 and 8-0 in the Big Eight. Colorado was second with a 5-2 record, while KU now was 4-3.

It was shortly after this game that sportscasters began to speculate on the All-American status of K-State's play-making guard, Matuszak. California's Pete Newell said, "Matuszak is the key to the club." Oklahoma State's Hank Iba often commented on what a force Matuszak was, and Missouri's Sparky Stalcup called him, "One of the greatest little men I've ever seen." Assistant Coach Howie Shannon thought he was definitely All-American and became downright agitated when it was pointed out that Matuszak averaged only 9.3 points per game. "He could be averaging 20 a game if he weren't so unselfish," Shannon argued.

On Valentine's Day, Oklahoma State invaded Manhattan and they were impressive, but even their 46.3% shooting and their constant press weren't enough. The Wildcats continued their winning drive for the conference title, winning their 9th game with no losses in the conference. The win moved Kansas State to a 19-1 record. It was Oklahoma State's 11th loss in 19 games and their conference mark was now 2-6.

Tex said of the game, "…for overall performance this was our best night." A sportswriter called it "a good whipping."

The Wildcats continued to roar as they easily defeated Oklahoma on their court by 20 points only a few days later. That took the Cats' successive wins to 16 and boosted their season record to 20-1 and their Big Eight mark to 10-0. All that was needed to even the tie for the championship was another win. The team had a chance to do that in their next game with Oklahoma State in Stillwater.

The game was on television and the arena was full, but the Oklahoma State Cowboys just couldn't pull off an upset. The Wildcats from Kansas State were still churning out victories. Both coaches conceded that their team "played as fine a game as we are capable of playing." The final score was Wildcats 62, Cowboys 50.

In winning their 17th straight game, and 11th in the conference, the Wildcats cinched a bid to the NCAA Regionals. Colorado was the only team that could tie them and K-State had beaten them twice, so there would be no coin toss decision.

The Cats were in the final stretch. They had won the coveted conference championship when, during the past week, Nebraska had rolled over Colorado. And, even more exciting, they were now ranked #2 in both national polls. But first they had to finish the season, and KU – their nemesis – was next. KU was looking toward being #2 in the conference and they desperately needed this win. They were tied with Colorado and Oklahoma. K-State had been the victor in the previous meeting, but that was on their home court, a distinct advantage as any Big Eight fan would tell you.

Going into the game, the Wildcats appeared strong. Boozer had already riddled the individual records for K-State. To this date he had 1,548 points, passing the previous high of 1,185 by Jack Parr. He had also toppled Parr's record with 754 points against conference opponents. Parr's had been 591. Tex was fully aware that last year's team had seemed to let down after they had cinched the title, but he didn't think this group would. This was a tightly bound group, full of spirit and determination. They had beaten the odds already.

In a spirited battle, the teams kept scrambling for the lead, but K-State's shooting was more accurate and their hustle was evident. Both teams tallied fouls as they kept pushing for the victory. The score at the buzzer indicated to their fans that the Wildcats were dominant over the Jayhawks: 87-77. The Cats had recorded their 18th straight win.

On March 7th the Missouri Tigers came to Manhattan to play, but evidently weren't ready for either the Wildcats or their exuberant fans. They were beaten easily in the first half by a mighty K-State team that was shooting with great accuracy. The Tigers were on the losing end of an overwhelming victory, 108-69, in front of a crowd estimated at 10,500 and a regional television audience. They all got to see as much of Winter's reserve team as they did of the regulars, and those reserves were definitely impressive.

This marked K-State's 19th consecutive win and they brought their conference mark to 13-0 and their season record to 23-1. Missouri now was 2-11 in conference play.

Tex felt badly about the score. He said they hadn't intended to break any records. He knew that Sparky Stalcup, Missouri's coach, was in his worst season in 13 years and was being given a rough time by fans and alumni. Sparky, however, didn't feel that the Cats had tried to "pour it on." He said, "I feel K-State is the #1 team in the country. They've got everything you want in a basketball team." It was the first time that Sparky had seen an adversary score 100 points against him. Tex praised Price and called Boozer an All-American in more ways than just on the court. He praised the entire team. One of the startling facts was that *mostly reserves had played the entire 2nd half!*

The next week found the Wildcats on top in national rankings and on their way to a clean sweep in the Big Eight. Not since 1946 had that been accomplished and then it was by KU. On the minds of everyone was how the Cats would handle the pressure going into the Midwest Regionals the following week. Coach Winter acknowledged that his team had let him down after winning the conference championship last year by losing games going into the regionals, but he was confident that it wouldn't happen again.

"This is the most consistent team, both in competition and in practice I've ever coached and I hope we won't have a bad letdown this time." Winter went on to say he was very confident of the ability of Bob Boozer, a scoring ace averaging 25.2 points a game, and of Matuszak's play-making skills. He went on to cite all the team members as outstanding contributors.

Although K-State was #1 in the UPI ratings, with Kentucky in the 2nd spot, the AP had the teams reversed. Both polls showed Cincinnati in #3 position, and the next three on the lists were Mississippi State, North Carolina, and Michigan State.

The Wildcat statistics to date for the year showed that Boozer, Frank, Matuszak, and Long were shooting in the 40-42% range. Mickey Heinz, a go-to man on the reserve squad, was averaging 47%, and Joe Vader, the football player who came to help out when Tex needed to fill his bench, was averaging a big 100%. He had made the only field goal he'd attempted! Boozer was easily leading in rebounds with 257. Following were Wally Frank with 190 and Cedric Price, who had come on board late, with 139. Douglas was next with 125 and Matuszak had 106. It was a balanced effort, without a doubt.

Balance seemed to be the key. An analogy is often made about "one bad apple spoiling the bunch." Is then the converse true, that a good attitude becomes infectious? Can grit and determination overcome perhaps-superior talent? Do people or circumstances or attitudes make a *team*? Here was a team made up of young men who had sought the chance to play basketball, a disparate group that forged a team and made history for their school. When the regulars played until they were either too tired or were ahead by a wide margin, they passed the baton to the guys who sat on the bench most of the time. And those teammates – Bill Guthridge, Mickey Heinz, Bob Graham, Gary Balding, Glenn Hamilton, Jerry Johnson, Joe Vader, Glen Long (finally recovered from his injury), and Sonny Ballard (in the first semester) – never let them down.

One sportswriter who addressed the fortunes of the Wildcats since Tex had taken the reins said the K-State record was particularly noteworthy. In the past four seasons the Wildcats had taken three conference titles, and finished the previous year in 2nd place. The fact was, he said, the team was comprised of athletes who had not been high on any school's recruiting list, and many of the players had come to K-State because they did not receive scholarship offers from anywhere else. But once the players were at K-State, Winter and his assistants, Howie Shannon and Ernie Barrett, molded them into consistent winners. Winter worked them on fundamentals, and gave them an intense desire to succeed. Though there might be great seasons ahead, it would be a rare accomplishment for a team to post a 21-1 record again, he said.

March 9th marked the final game in Manhattan and the final game for the seniors on the squad. That night the three seniors, Boozer, Matuszak, and Holwerda, were given a standing ovation by the crowd as they were introduced before the regular introductions. It was a very sentimental and emotional time for all the players, as is every final season game, but this was K-State at its finest, and the fans let them know how much they had appreciated their efforts.

And, the Cats came out to play, drubbing the Nebraska team 76-54. It was their last conference game, meaning they had gone through the season undefeated in the Big Eight. Nebraska didn't go down easily, though, and fought hard throughout the contest.

The victory set a new record, as K-State became the first team to finish the conference season unbeaten since Kansas did it in the old Big Six in 1946. It was a memorable night for the very biased fans that had packed the field house.

As the Cats prepared for the regional games, both national sports polls now ranked them #1 in the nation. That made them the "team to beat." Tex and the players knew they would have a tough time in the games facing them. They remembered their poor showing in the finals the year before, and hoped to redeem themselves. "Everybody knows we played poorly at Louisville last year," Winter said. "Our kids know it better than anybody and we are anxious to prove we can play well." (In the Midwest Regionals the year before, K-State won over Cincinnati and Oklahoma State, but was humbled by Seattle and Temple in the Final Four.)

"We've got our work cut out for us in the regionals," Winter commented. "I watched Cincinnati beat Wichita last Saturday and they are great. Oscar Robertson is an All-American and so is this guy, Ralph Davis. There isn't a better pair on one team in the country.

"At this stage I'd say our team is about on a par with last season's team, maybe not as strong on a given night. But we sank fast after clinching the championship last year." Winter reflected on the Wildcats' only loss during the season, to Brigham Young, on the home stretch of a three-game swing out west in December. "Maybe BYU did us a favor," he said. "All I have to do now is say 'remember Brigham Young' and the guys go out fighting."

Kansas State would lay the nation's longest winning streak and their number #1 national ranking on the line against DePaul, while the other pair, Texas Christian vs. Cincinnati, would showcase Robertson – the nation's scoring leader, with a 33.2 average. The eliminations involved 16 teams who would play over the weekend, narrowing the field to four teams who would compete for the showdown again in Louisville. Five of the top ten teams from the Associated Press final poll and four of the All-Americas would be featured. The five teams were #1 Kansas State, #2 Kentucky, #5 Cincinnati, #6 Michigan State, and #10 West Virginia. The All-America players were Oscar Robertson from Cincinnati, Bob Boozer from Kansas State, Jerry West from West Virginia, and Johnny Cox of Kentucky.

Exactly one year earlier, Kansas State had met Cincinnati in the regionals and had beaten them, only to go on to the nationals where they placed a disappointing fourth.

MIDWEST REGIONALS
@ LAWRENCE vs. DEPAUL

DePaul's coach, Ray Meyer, had assessed the Wildcats after the K-State vs. Nebraska game. "Kansas State has a very fine basketball team," he said. "They're terrific on the boards and a good, well-rounded team. Anybody can hurt you. They're as different as night and day from the Kansas State team we saw in the national finals last year."

Coach Tex Winter didn't think the Cats had looked particularly good in their game with Nebraska, but he was happy with the victory and proud that his club had become the first to go though the conference season unbeaten since 1946. And, too, this conference now included more teams.

"It's a wonderful thing," Winter said. "Maybe some Big Eight school will do as well some day, but they will never do any better." Winter had emphasized to his team that they were now in the fourth season of play, following (1) the non-conference season, (2) the pre-season tournament, and (3) the Big Eight season. "Nothing we've done up to this point will help us. We've got to go out with revived enthusiasm and vitality to do the job we want to do. The teams we'll be meeting will be tougher than the teams we've been playing."

DePaul could have been one of those teams. They had proved victorious against three teams who had qualified for the NCAA playoffs. They were not as big as K-State, but were tough competitors.

However, K-State came out charging against DePaul and had them down the first 10 minutes. At that point the Cats were ahead 28-13. Three minutes later the spread had reached 40-17 and Wally Frank was hot, scoring 15 points by then. K-State started picturing the 100-point mark, and they made it when reserve player Bob Graham scored on a short jump shot, bringing a rousing cheer from the partisan crowd. K-State's final score of 102-70 set a new regional record.

The game showed a balanced effort for the Wildcats. Frank scored with great accuracy from 15-20 feet, and finished the game with 23 points. Boozer added 16, his lowest of the season. Douglas hit 15 points, while Cedric Price got 14, and Jim Holwerda had 11. The Wildcats hit a scorching 47% from the field.

DePaul's coach, Ray Meyer, said after the game, "We have a pretty good little team, but we're out of business against a good big team like that." When asked to compare K-State against some of the top teams that DePaul had played that year, Meyer said, "No comparison. . . not on the basis of tonight's game, anyway. We never were even in this game tonight."

K-State used its height and fast-break ability to stun the DePaul team. Guard Matuszak showed off ball control as he dribbled inside, outside, and around the Chicago team. Caught in the backcourt, he dribbled behind his back, around his legs, and about every way possible and DePaul couldn't stop him. Douglas moved from guard to forward and back, showing his role as a driver. He broke quickly on the fast break and grabbed six rebounds. Frank and Douglas had their finest game of the season. The starters were out for a good portion of the game, but the reserves held their own and kept up the scoring pace.

Starters for the game were Frank, Boozer, Price, Matuszak, and Douglas. Reserves were used freely and the scoring was scattered throughout the entire bench. Besides the scorers mentioned above, Matuszak and Heinz each had six, Guthridge and Johnson had four, Graham two, and Long one.

Vs. CINCINNATI

And so it was, Cincinnati again would be the foe to beat. The Bearcats were determined to win this time and go on to the NCAA tournament that had been denied them last year. K-State too, had an agenda: they wanted to show that the final poll that made them #1 in the country was well earned. They had not held up well last year and they were determined to avenge themselves now.

Ill-timed bad luck, though, again inflicted its damage on one of the Cats' starting five. Matuszak woke up the morning of the game with a rash, and he had a hard time even moving. The trainer and team doctor were called and, after an examination, ordered him to rest the entire day. He was instructed not to even attend any pre-game meetings. However, he mentally prepared himself in hopes that he could play that night.

Both teams showed up ready to play – K-State's starting five in place – and the game proved both rough and brilliant. At one point officials had to stop the action to warn both squads about the excessive contact taking place. The Wildcats were behind 23-28 in the first half when Boozer went on a scoring rampage. He hit layups and jump shots in the final six minutes of the first half as Robertson tried to guard him. K-State pulled to a 41-39 half-time lead. Matuszak provided the 2-point margin with his patented steal and layup just before the first half ended.

In the second half, K-State, paced by Boozer's 32 points, suddenly lost control of the game with 4 minutes remaining. Cincinnati's Lanfried hit a layup and as he shot, Jim Holwerda slammed into Robertson. Robertson hit two free throws and the Bearcats suddenly went from a 67-58 deficit to a 71-68 lead, and they never trailed again.

Robertson hit a jump shot and the score was 73-68 with 3:20 remaining. Two field goals by Wally Frank and a layup by Boozer pulled the Cats to within 1 point. But the Bearcats raced to a 83-74 advantage before K-State could score again. The final score was 85-75, Cincy's favor.

The game had been close as the teams traded baskets, but Cincinnati hit 41% from the field, compared to K-State's 31%. Boozer was the top scorer with his 32 points, while Robertson scored 24 and probably accounted for at least that many more with his great feeds to teammates. Cincy's Tenwick, 6'6" center, tallied 22 points.

K-State played 9 men, while Cincinnati fielded only 7. The rebounding advantage only slightly belonged to K-State with 53 rebounds compared to 52 by the Bearcats.

Others providing points for the Wildcats were Price with 11, Frank ten, Matuszak eight, Holwerda six, Guthridge and Douglas three each, and Heinz (who did a great job defensively on Robertson after Price fouled out) scored two.

***

At their annual basketball banquet, the crowd paid special tribute to the departing seniors: Bob Boozer, Don Matuszak, and Jim Holwerda. When those three were sophomores, Tex had said, "This was a good season, but the best is yet to come." It was a prophecy he could not repeat at *this* banquet.

Following the Cincinnati game, Matuszak had returned to Manhattan where doctors at Student Health hospitalized him with the diagnosis of mononucleosis. He was discharged after a week and joined Boozer to play in two post-season All-Star games.

Sportswriters predicted that the combination of Boozer and Matuszak would always set the standard – the deadly shooting of Boozer paired with the great playmaking and ball-handling of Matuszak. Holwerda had often been recognized as one of the most accurate shooters on the team. He had lost some of his accuracy this season, but he never lost his driving ambition to do better. He had practiced intensely, and had often made the outside shots that make a difference.

Boozer had again made the 1st team consensus All-America list,* the first K-Stater to make the prestigious first team and now named to the list a second time. **Matuszak received All-American honors.** Bob was drafted in the first round by Cincinnati, and Don went in the 8th round, also to Cincy.

There will undoubtedly be some confusion about the terms "All-America," "honorable-mention All-America," "All-American honors," and "*consensus* All-America." "Best of the best" lists were compiled by a variety of groups, organizations, and magazines. In the 1950s, lists by the Associated Press (sports writers and broadcasters) and United Press International (basketball coaches) were considered the most reliable. The National Collegiate Athletic Association adhered to a selected number of lists and kept mainly, during that decade, to the same ones – namely the AP, UPI, and others mentioned in this text.

In the 1940s the Helms Foundation (a bakery designated as the official bakery for the 1932 Olympics in Los Angeles) and Converse (the maker of basketball shoes) were two of the strong assessors. By 1948 neither of them were still on the officially recognized roster of list compilers. Madison Square Garden,

Argosy Magazine, and *True Magazine* also once produced lists.

A player might make it onto one list or many lists. It became customary to compile a list of the *consensus* selections, recognizing those players mentioned most often on the *selected* lists. At the heart of the matter is the fact that the consensus list is where the best players in the nation are listed.

If a player were mentioned by *any* group but not named to the *consensus* selection he could be referred to as receiving "All-American honors." If one of the leading groups named him as an honorable mention he could be referred to that way, or could be said to have won "All-American honors." The terms were mutually inclusive.

Matuszak was voted Honorary Captain, and for the 2nd year was voted Most Inspirational Player by his teammates, and also received the coveted Mike Ahearn Award as K-State's Athlete of the Year. It was the first time a basketball player had received the honor. Bebe Lee, the athletic director, announced, "His ability to spark the basketball team was exhibited in game after game throughout the season. His off-court conduct and cooperation have been equally outstanding." **Holwerda was awarded the trophy for the highest free throw accuracy, with 86% shooting.**

The 1st All Big Eight Team named that year included:
Bob Boozer, Kansas State
Don Matuszak, Kansas State
Arlen Clark, Oklahoma State
Bill Bridges, Kansas
Gerry Schroeder, Colorado

* Others on the 1st team All-America list for the 1958-59 season: Oscar Robertson (Cincinnati), Jerry West (West Virginia),

Bailey Howell (Mississippi State), and Johnny Cox (Kentucky). The second team was made up of Leo Byrd (Marshall), Johnny Green (Michigan State), Tom Hawkins (Notre Dame), Don Henron (Pittsburgh), and Alan Seiden (St. John's).

***

Thus, the Kansas State Wildcats ended their finest season in the school's history with a 25-2 record. Even though it would be Cincinnati that would take a 25-3 mark on to the NCAA finals in Louisville, the polls considered the entire season and the fact that the teams that led consistently had played some of the most competitive schedules. It was an obvious choice: **K-State was named by both the Associated Press and the United Press in the final poll of the season as <u>THE NUMBER ONE TEAM</u> in the nation.**

1958-59 Team – Voted #1 in the nation
Top row: *Ernie Barrett, Mickey Heinz, Cedric Price, Bob Boozer, Wally Frank, Steve Douglas.* **2nd Row:** *"Porky" Morgan, Glen Long, Joe Vader, Bob Graham, Jerry Johnson, Howie Shannon, Coach Tex Winter.* **Bottom Row:** *Gary Balding, Glenn Hamilton, Don Matuszak, Bill Guthridge, Jim Holwerda.*

The University of California, the team that K-State had beaten earlier, eventually won the tournament by defeating West Virginia. Others in the finals were Cincinnati and Louisville. However, the teams named by the final polls were #1-Kansas State, #2-Kentucky, #3-Mississippi State, #4-Bradley, and #5-Cincinnati. The alumni, students, and fans of K-State were overjoyed at the national publicity they received and the prestige that accompanied it.

The success had started in 1955-56 when a group of eager sophomores reported to Coach Tex Winter. They included Larry Fischer, Hayden Abbott, Don Richards, Jack Parr and Roy DeWitz. That was Tex's 3rd year of coaching; he had posted two consecutive seasons of 11-10. That team was able to post a record of 17-8. Some of the veterans on the team were Dick Stone, Pachin Vincens, and Fritz Schneider. Although they placed only 5th in the pre-season tournament, they eventually won the conference title. In the NCAA regionals, DeWitz was unable to play because of a broken foot. The Cats lost a hard-fought game to Oklahoma City 97-93.

The 1956-57 season brought Bob Boozer, Don Matuszak, and Jim Holwerda. That team took 2nd in the conference, finishing the season with a 15-8 advantage.

In 1957-58 Wally Frank entered the scene. He was a 6'8" forward with a deadly shot who became the "6th regular," and the team swept the Big Seven title, climbing to #1 in the nation before fate again hit them. After winning in the regionals against Cincinnati and Oscar Robertson, 83-80, the Cats were picked to go all the way to the national title. But a terrible illness struck one of the key players, and his teammates played below their ability as they floundered in confusion. They finished 4th in the tournament and 3rd and 4th in the national polls.

The team started the 1958-59 season with doubts from the fans and forecasters, but not from the players. They were fueled with determination and, fortunately, when football season was over, Cedric Price joined the team, giving Tex more options and a better balance of players.

A primary reason for the Wildcats' success during those two particularly outstanding seasons was the lack of super stars. Not one player among them could be called the star, and not one had been intensely recruited. Most of them came to Kansas State because it offered the only opportunity they had to play ball. Some players had other offers, but nothing better than K-State.

Under the guidance and discipline of Tex Winter and his assistants, Howie Shannon and Ernie Barrett, those players became great players. They had a sense of "team," and a burning desire to win. Their camaraderie was the magic ingredient. They believed in themselves, and they absolutely refused to lose.

Of the season, Tex said, "This is the greatest bunch of kids I have ever worked with. I can assure all of you that the season just completed has been the greatest experience of my life. This has been the easiest team to coach that a coach could ever hope to have."

As of this writing:

- Bob Boozer remains the only #1 consensus All-American basketball player named from Kansas State and he attained that prestigious honor two times, both in 1958 and 1959.*
- The 1958-59 basketball team is the only Kansas State team named Number 1 in the nation in both leading polls.

* Other K-Staters who have been named to consensus All-American status: Ernie Barrett, 2nd team, 1951; Dick Knostman, 2nd team, 1953; and Mitch Richmond, 2nd team, 1988.

Starters on the #1 team: *Boozer, Matuszak, and Frank with Coach Tex Winter*

RECAP OF THE GAMES

The games listed in bold print are included in the story. Details of the remaining games follow the season schedules.

1957-58 SCHEDULE

12/3/57	Texas Western @ Home
12/7/57	Indiana @ Bloomington
12/9/57	Purdue @ Lafayette
12/14/57	Iowa Univ. @ Home
12/16/57	Arkansas Univ. @ Fayetteville
12/20-21/57	Sunflower Classic
	vs. Univ. of California
	vs. Univ. of Washington
12/27-31	**Big 8 Pre-season Tournament @ Kansas City – Final Game**
1/6/58	Minnesota Univ. @ Home
1/11/58	Nebraska Univ. @ Home
1/18/58	Oklahoma Univ. @ Norman
1/25/58	Iowa State Univ. @ Ames
2/1/58	Colorado Univ. @ Home
2/3/58	**Kansas Univ. @ Lawrence**
2/8/58	Iowa State Univ. @ Home
2/15/58	Colorado Univ. @ Boulder

2/22/58	Missouri Univ. @ Columbia
2/25/58	Oklahoma Univ. @ Home
3/1/58	**Missouri Univ. @ Home**
3/3/58	**Nebraska Univ. @ Lincoln**
3/8/58	**Kansas Univ. @ Home**
3/14-15/58	**Midwest Regionals @ Lawrence**
	vs. Cincinnati
	vs. Oklahoma State
FINAL FOUR	**NCAA Tournament @ Louisville, KY**
	vs. Seattle
	vs. Temple

1958-59 SCHEDULE

12/1/58	Purdue Univ. @ Home
12/6/58	Indiana @ Home
12/12/58	California Univ. @ Berkeley
12/13/58	San Francisco @ San Francisco
12/15/58	Brigham Young Univ. @ Provo
12/19/58	**Sunflower Classic**:
	vs. North Carolina State
	vs. St. Joseph's
12/26-30	**Big 8 Pre-season Tournament**
	@ Kansas City
1/8/59	Iowa State @ Ames
1/10/59	Colorado Univ. @ Home
1/12/59	Oklahoma Univ. @ Home
1/17/59	**Missouri@ Columbia**
1/26/59	Iowa State @ Home
1/31/59	South Dakota State @ Home
2/2/59	Nebraska Univ. @ Lincoln

2/7/59	Colorado Univ. @ Boulder
2/11/59	Kansas Univ. @ Home
2/14/59	Oklahoma State Univ. @ Home
2/16/59	Oklahoma University @ Norman
2/21/59	Oklahoma State Univ. @ Stillwater
2/27/59	Kansas Univ. @ Lawrence
3/7/59	Missouri Univ. @ Home
3/9/59	Nebraska Univ. @ Home
3/13-14/59	**Midwest Regionals @ Lawrence** **vs. DePaul** **vs. Cincinnati**

1957-58 GAMES

Vs. TEXAS WESTERN (12/3/57)
@ HOME
WIN 76-31

On December 3rd, the season opened with Texas Western in Ahearn Field House. A noisy crowd of 9,000 witnessed the lop-sided game. The win was impressive: 76-31, with Parr and Boozer leading the scoring and rebounding. Parr had 18 points and 8 rebounds, while Boozer put in 11 points and grabbed 11 rebounds. It was the most successful K-State opener since 1949 when Nebraska was held to 28 points.

Texas Western's Charlie Brown, a 6'0" forward, was their

outstanding player, and he and John Sanders, a 6'3" forward, each had nine points. Brown also led with his team in rebounds, snaring nine.

K-State led by 21 points, 37-16, at halftime. With 12:37 on the clock, the Cats were on top 47-22. Then, for 9 ½ minutes Texas Western failed to score as the Cats pumped in 14 more. Texas Western tried their stall game as Coach Winter cleared the bench. The Cat reserves continued to widen the margin, leading 66-24 with 3:58 on the clock, then 72-24 with 2:55 left in the game.

K-State shot 31-70 from the field for 44.3%, while Texas Western had only 12 for 50 for 24%. On the free throw line the Cats had 14 for 22 and Texas Western was 7 for 13.

Others scoring for K-State were Abbott and DeWitz each with 10, Frank with eight, Fischer put in six, Plagge had three, and Matuszak, Holwerda, Douglas, and Laude added two points each. Also playing were Ballard, Long, and Guthridge.

It was a glorious beginning!

Vs. INDIANA (12/7/57)
@ HOME
WIN 66-61

The Cats felt good about their great opening game, but there was pressure with this next one: Indiana had whipped K-State in their last five games, four of them by 20 points or more. Indiana was coming into this game having just been beaten by Ohio University 76-68, but they were still rated at least as strong as last year when they had tied for the Big 10 title with Michigan State. Archie Dees, 6'8", played both as forward and center for Indiana and was their scoring ace. He had led the Big 10 last year with 25 points a game average and was the Big 10 Most Valuable Player.

Tex started the same five as in the opener. Boozer was the leading Wildcat scorer with 27 points and 19 rebounds, while Parr had 16 points and 13 rebounds. Indiana led at times by as much as 11 points in the first half. The Hoosiers were hitting at a 42.9% and K-State couldn't seem to find the basket at times. But, by intermission K-State came back to within two points, at 34-36. The lead changed hands four times in the 2nd half with Wally Frank laying one up with 1:56 remaining and that put the Cats ahead to stay.

Vs. PURDUE (12/9/57)
@ LAFAYETTE, IND.
WIN 79-73

The Cats faced another tough Big 10 opponent several nights later at Purdue in front of 10,000 loud and screaming fans. Boozer again led the scoring with 25, while sophomore Wally Frank came in with a surprise 18, getting 12 of those in the second half. Jack Parr had 14.

Purdue had the lead with 8:07 left when Parr committed his fifth foul and Purdue made the free throw to put the score at 59-60. K-State went ahead to stay at 61-60 on a tip-in by Boozer with 7:43 remaining. Frank got two field goals, then a free throw by Boozer gave the Cats a six-point margin. Purdue closed within three points with 46 seconds left on the clock. Glen Long hit a layup to give the Cats a five-point gap, but Purdue's Greve countered with a set shot. Then, with 17 seconds to go, Matuszak swished a free throw for a 77-73 score and DeWitz put in the clincher for a final of 79-73. K-State had 39 rebounds to Purdue's 33. The Cats led the field goal percentage with 42.8% to Purdue's 39.1%.

Others scoring for the Cats were Matuszak with six, Long and DeWitz with five each, Abbott with four, and Holwerda had two.

Vs. IOWA UNIVERSITY (12/14/57)
@ HOME
WIN 86-69

The team was beginning to generate more and more fans. Over 11,000 people crowded into Ahearn to watch the Cats win their fourth game in a row and their third one over Big 10 opponents. Iowa kept close behind during most of the game, trailing only 35-42 at halftime, and then by only two points, 58-60, with 9:19 left in the game. But, in the last seven minutes K-State scored 17 while Iowa only made seven. Parr was high with 25 points, Boozer had 19, and Frank scored 14. Shooting percentages were in K-State's favor with 44.8% to Iowa's 33.8%. Rebounds were also dominated by K-State, 48-38. Tex commented after the game, "This was the second time we've used a zone defense. We figured it would slow them down and cut out some fouling. It worked most of the time." Also scoring were DeWitz with 11, Matuszak eight, Abbott five, and Douglas four.

Following this game, K-State rose in both the AP and UPI polls to third. North Carolina was ranked #1 and Kansas #2.

Vs. ARKANSAS (12/16/57)
@ FAYETTEVILLE
WIN 63-48

With both teams playing tight zone defenses, K-State and Arkansas played a slow and low-scoring game – the lowest-scoring game for the Wildcats so far that season. At halftime K-State led 36-26. The Cats pulled away, however, in the second half, leading 50-36 with ten minutes left. This gave Coach Winter a chance to put in the reserves and it soon became apparent that they too had strength, as Douglas, Laude, and Ballard all hit field goals in the final minutes.

High scorer was Boozer with 19 points; Parr had 12, DeWitz nine, Abbott and Frank each had seven, Matuszak scored three, and Laude, Ballard, and Douglas each had two points.

SUNFLOWER CLASSIC
Vs. UNIVERSITY OF CALIFORNIA (12/20/57)
@ LAWRENCE
WIN 58-44

California had K-State down 15-8 early in the game and battled the Cats throughout the game. Finally, with his team leading by only one point, the scoreboard reading 39-38, Boozer went on a shooting spree. He hit a one-hander from the corner and two hooks from the free throw line, and very quickly the tally was 47-38. It was Boozer and Hayden Abbott who provided most of the offensive spark with Boozer putting in 22 and Abbott 18. At halftime the Wildcats had a lead of only 28-26 and the game continued close until the last ten minutes.

K-State shot only 35% and the California team, with a very cold second half, wound up shooting only 20%. The Cats had played a man-to-man defense in the first half, but came out in a zone after the intermission, seemingly stifling the Bears.

Others in the scoring column were DeWitz and Matuszak with six each, Frank with four, and Parr hit two free throws.

SUNFLOWER CLASSIC
Vs. UNIVERSITY OF WASHINGTON (12/21/57)
@ HOME
WIN 70-63

In a fairly easy effort, the Wildcats had the Washington Huskies down 67-48 with nine minutes still to play, prompting Coach Winter to send in his reserves. The Huskies fought back and trailed by only nine, at 67-58, with two minutes to go. Tex then put the starters back in and wrapped it up easily.

Bob Boozer was the game's top scorer with 22 points. He sank 14 of 17 of his free throws. Don Matuszak had his best night of the season as far as scoring, with 14 points. Hayden Abbott had 10, Roy DeWitz put in nine, and Jack Parr had eight.

Parr had been treated for an upset stomach that day and was not playing at his peak. But he did a good defensive job on Doug Smart, the Huskies' top scorer, limiting him to 15 points, only five of those in the second half.

The Wildcats led at halftime 41-27, took the score up to 61-42, and finally, with the scoreboard reading 67-48, the reserves came in and the Huskies managed to put in 15 points to the Cats 3. The outcome was never in doubt.

Vs. MINNESOTA (1/6/58)
@ HOME
WIN 72-71

It was obvious that Minnesota was determined and gave the Wildcats all they could handle. The Cats led at halftime by only 44-43. The second half was close, but Minnesota led most of the time and had the lead by six points with only 6:15 to go. The Cats finally gained the lead when Matuszak hit a layup with 3:25 to go in the game. He was fouled and sank his free throw, making the score 70-67. Then DeWitz fouled with 1:04 on the clock. Minnesota made the one and one shots, leaving the score then at 70-69.

The Cats took the ball out of bounds and a long downcourt pass caught Abbott all alone for a layup to make it 72-69. Minnesota player, Ron Johnson, hit a jump shot with 41 seconds to bring them within one point. Abbott was fouled with 20 seconds remaining, but missed the shot. Minnesota brought the ball down and lost it out of bounds, ending the game by a squeaking one point. Statistics for Minnesota were 41% on field goals and 70% from the line, compared to K-State's 32% on field goals and 69% from the line. K-State, however, dominated in rebounds, 56-44. Boozer again dominated the scoring with 27 points, Matuszak had 14, Abbott 12, Frank eight, Parr seven, and DeWitz four.

K-state was now ready to begin the conference play. They would face their first foe, Nebraska, in only five more days.

Vs. NEBRASKA (1/11/58)
@ HOME
WIN 74-59

The Wildcats faced Nebraska on their home court to kick off their conference schedule. It was not a hard-fought contest, as Nebraska was overpowered on the boards.

K-State had 67 rebounds to Nebraska's 37. Parr had one of his best games, adding 20 points and 20 rebounds. He held the Nebraska post man, 6'9" Allen Graves, to 0 for 3 from the field and Graves made only 1 of 2 free throws for his only point of the game.

Abbott grabbed 13 rebounds while DeWitz got 12.

Nebraska kept the score close during the first half, trailing only 33-41 at intermission. But with only 7:30 left in the game they were down by 5. All the Wildcats who played were in the scoring column. Guards DeWitz and Matuszak had nine and six points, respectively. Frank hit for eight, while Holwerda played a sharp floor game and sank two shots, and Fischer added five points. No accurate box score was available.

Tex expressed his concern about the lack of outside shooting, pointing out that the guards scored mostly on close shots. But he was optimistic about Parr, saying, "Jack should be on his way now." The coach noted that the Cats were going to have to play their best game of the season to win over Oklahoma in their next game.

Nebraska's coach, Jerry Bush, was impressed with Frank. "His being around the next two years will really help K-State basketball."

Vs. OKLAHOMA (1/18/58)
@ NORMAN
WIN 64-60

Just as Tex had predicted, Oklahoma came to play ball. K-State entered the game ranked now at #2, while Oklahoma also had a national ranking of #14.

Oklahoma led most of the first half and at intermission were ahead 32-29. The Oklahoma Sooners were out-rebounding the Cats, but free throws kept the Wildcats in the game. At one point during the first half, K-State went 10 minutes without scoring. In the 2nd half after several ties, K-State went ahead on a tip-in by Boozer with 7:17 remaining on the clock. K-state capitalized on free throws, putting in 78.8% against the Sooners' 47.6%.

Jim Holwerda was on the injury list with a sprained ankle, but Tex didn't play too many other than his "starting 6" during the game. Boozer was high scorer with 21 points, followed by the Sooners' Bill Hammond who had 16. Other Wildcats scoring were Parr with 15, Abbott and Frank each with eight, DeWitz with seven, and Matuszak with five.

Vs. IOWA STATE (1/25/58)
@ AMES
WIN 64-54

Going into this game Tex was a bit pessimistic. Iowa State, always a tough competitor, had played the Cats to two overtimes last season, splitting the wins. Each team was back with good strength and a winning desire. Iowa State had just come off a loss to Colorado and were 2-1 in conference play. They needed to stay in contention. K-State was 2-0 and wanted to keep the pressure on their chief rival, Kansas, who had lost a game and was now 2-1.

The Wildcats overwhelmed Iowa State's Cyclones on the Ames court and moved a full game ahead of Kansas in the Big 7 race with a 3-1 record. As usual, the Cats waged a well-balanced attack. Roy DeWitz was the scoring ace in this game, accounting for 18 points. He also held Lyle Frahm, the 6'2" guard, to a total of four points. Frahm had been averaging 11.6 per game.

K-State took a commanding 17-7 point lead by midway in the first half, due mainly to DeWitz and Parr, who contributed 15 points. Iowa State came within 5 at 20-25. Then DeWitz and Frank rolled in more baskets to put the Wildcats in a 32-23 halftime lead.

The second half started slowly, but Parr, Boozer, Frank, and Abbott controlled the backboards while DeWitz and Matuszak pressed on defense and the Cats took over again with a 16-point lead. The Cyclones almost caught up, making it 33-28, but K-State started a scoring surge. Abbott found his range and hit three straight jump shots and the Cats moved to a 47-33 lead with 10 minutes on the clock. Using a man-to-man defense, the Wildcats held the Cyclones to very few good shots. Iowa State did make some long-range buckets but was never able to close the gap.

No box scores were available.

Vs. COLORADO (2/1/58)
@ HOME
WIN 83-54

Bob Boozer found his scoring touch, leading the Wildcats to an easy victory against the Colorado Buffaloes, putting in 28 points. Jack Parr followed with 19. The Cats hit a hot 50.7% of their field goals, a total of 34 of 67, their best shooting of the season. Colorado hit only 29 out of 65 for a 29.2% average. K-State also led in rebounding, 56-39, with Jack Parr grabbing 10. From the free throw line, K-State hit 69.6% while the Buffaloes hit 62.5%.

The Cats led at halftime 44-31, but both teams decided to switch to zone defense the second half, leaving Colorado wide open for the Wildcats' relentless speed.

In the last five minutes of the game, K-State's reserve unit of four sophomores and one junior outscored Colorado 12-4. This game was K-State's fourth victory in the Big Seven. They remained undefeated in the conference. Their ranking was #3 nationally.

Others scoring for the Cats were Frank with nine, Abbott with eight, and Matuszak, Ballard, and Holwerda with four each, Long with three, and DeWitz and Douglas each with two.

Vs. IOWA STATE (2/8/58)
@ HOME
WIN 77-70

It was a record-setting night as Kansas State made it a 16-1 season, topping the 1947-48 team's 15 wins. Jack Parr broke the school record for all-time total points. Dick Knostman, a former All-America player, had achieved 1,083 points. On this night Parr reached 1,090. But the game win did not come easily, for the Cyclones refused time and again to be put away.

The Cats held the lead by two points, at 61-59, with four minutes on the clock. Then the teams started exchanging fouls and free throws. K-State was hot on the line and hit shot after shot. Both teams hit at 85% of their charity shots, but it was down the stretch that the Cats made them count.

Each time the Cats got ahead, the Cyclones would come back. The score was tied seven times during the second half. Jim Holwerda came off the bench to give the Cats a lift midway in the second. He hit three straight, long arching set shots, and each one put the Cats ahead by two. The team never trailed after that. Abbot made the final bucket, a lay-up with two seconds remaining.

Boozer was high point man with 20 points, Parr had 18, Abbott put in 16, Dewitz had nine, Matuszak and Holwerda each scored six, and Frank put in two.

Vs. COLORADO (2/15/58)
@ BOULDER
WIN 68-62

Kansas State was at the halfway mark in their conference schedule as they journeyed to Boulder for what they hoped would be an easy victory. However, the Colorado Buffaloes had other ideas and gave the Wildcats all they could handle. Again, it was Jim Holwerda who came off the bench to spark the winning rally with three jump shots to give the Cats some breathing room. Those needed baskets came after the game was 14 minutes into the second half. The first half had been ragged, but the Cats had gone into intermission with a lead of 32-30. The Buffaloes, in the cellar position in the conference, fought for rebounds under the basket and gave the Wildcats a shooting performance that caught the Cats off-guard. Both teams hit 44% from the field in the first half, and final tallies were 47.2% for the Cats and 46% for the Buffaloes.

The score was tied at 46 when Holwerda entered the game. He hit his first jump shot, making it 48-46, and Boozer followed with his first jump shot to make it 50-46. This seemed to give the Cats new life and Holwerda and Boozer each hit two more shots, almost putting the game out of reach. The last few minutes seemed to erupt into a brawl as fans booed calls against their teams. Both Sox Walseth, Colorado's coach, and Roy DeWitz, K-State guard, received technicals. Colorado did not give up, still operating its passing and cutting offense, and had narrowed the Cats' lead to 59-53 with only 3:23 on the clock. Two free throws by Matuszak and another dunker by Boozer moved the Cats to a 63-53 advantage. The final score was 68-62.

Boozer hit for 19 points, Parr for 14, Abbott at 13, Matuszak had seven, Holwerda and DeWitz each had six, and Frank put in three.

Vs. MISSOURI (2/22/58)
@ COLUMBIA
WIN 82-61

In an overpowering show of force, Kansas State left little doubt why they were now #1 in national ranking as they defeated the Missouri Tigers 82-61. It was K-State's eighth conference victory, with no losses. While the Cats were taking the win on this evening, KU was being handed a defeat by Nebraska in Lincoln, putting the Cats two and one-half games ahead of Kansas in the Big 7 race. Overall, K-State was now 18-1, with only four more conference games to play. Three were scheduled on their home court where, hopefully, that factor would play to their advantage. The fans were always considered a major force in their victories.

Missouri went out in front with an 11-7 lead in the first five minutes, but K-State took control after that. At halftime, the Cats led 38-33 and then bolted to a 47-35 score and coasted into an easy victory.

Once again Boozer led the scoring with 20 points and Parr was right behind with 18. Kansas State shot 50% from the field, making 33 out of 66 attempts. Missouri made only 18 of its 60 shots for a 30% average. Boozer also grabbed 16 rebounds, Parr and DeWitz snared seven each, and Matuszak five. Abbott scored 13 points, Matuszak 13, Frank six, DeWitz four, and Long, Holwerda, Ballard, and Richards two each.

The victory kept the Cats' hold on #1, but they just barely edged out West Virginia, with 574 points to West Virginia's 563. The 75 sportswriters and sportscasters who voted gave West Virginia the most first place votes, 22, with the Cats receiving 17 and Cincinnati 14. In fourth place was San Francisco, and Temple was now fifth. Kansas had slid down to 10th place.

Vs. OKLAHOMA UNIV. (2/25/58)
@ HOME
WIN 68-51

With their defeat of Oklahoma in this game, the Wildcats could wrap up the conference title. K-State remained undefeated in eight league games, so mathematically all contenders were out of the race. Kansas suffered its second straight upset, losing to Iowa State 48-42. The Jayhawks' record in the league stood at 6-4 with two games remaining.

And K-State clinched it! With a final score of 68-51, Kansas State claimed the championship crown! The Wildcats now held an overall 19-1 record, their only defeat to KU in the holiday tournament.

The victory prize came on Coach Tex Winter's 36th birthday. With a big smile spread over his face he said, "If anyone had told me before the season started that we would have the championship clinched with 3 games remaining, I would have suggested they have their head examined. Winning nine in a row in this conference is an almost unbelievable feat."

The Sooners played a good man-to-man defense the first half – at halftime they were down only two points, 28-30. Boozer again led scoring with 23 points, followed by Parr with 17 points before he left the game with a sprained ankle. Winter said the injury wasn't serious and that he thought Jack would be ready to play in next week's game against Missouri.

Others scoring were DeWitz and Matuszak with 10 each, Holwerda with four, Frank three, and Long one. Free throws accounted for 13 of Boozer's 23 points.

Winter wouldn't comment on the team's chances in the tournament. More than likely it would be a contest with Cincinnati, as they were the favorite in the Missouri Valley league. Doyle Parrack, OU's coach, said about K-State, "Let's put it this way. They're not overrated. I hope they win it. Man for man they are the best team we have played."

1958-59 GAMES

Vs. PURDUE (12/1/58)
@ HOME
WIN 96-83

The Wildcats were off to a slow start and had scored only 18 points at halftime, 12 from free throws and only three field goals.

Boozer came back to lead a second-half attack which left the Boilermakers far behind and in big foul trouble. However, Purdue was still in the game with 11 minutes on the clock. Boozer and Matuszak then combined to score 22 straight points (Boozer with 10, Matuszak with 12) and the scoreboard read K-State 74, Purdue 60 – putting the game out of the Boilermakers' reach with four minutes left. It was definitely Boozer's night as he scored a total of 45 points and hauled in 16 rebounds.

Glen Long, vying for a starting position, also led the initiative in the opening of the second half by making two jump shots, relieving some of the defensive pressure on Boozer. Coach Winter had high praise for his team, calling it a "mid-season game…the best I've ever seen in an opener." Winter pointed to the key factors: the Wildcats' conditioning and Purdue's trouble with fouls. "We just wore them down; conditioning played a big part," he said. "And they were hurt when they had to take [starters] Merriweather and Elson out in the second half."

Tex said of Glen Long's play, "I wasn't surprised. Long has looked real good in practice. He's a real fine board man and has good speed, and is a good scrambler."

Winter pointed out that the contest was one in which a "scrambler" would stand out, and Wally Frank was more of a deliberate player. This was not his best game, according to Winter, because he does better in a different mode of play. He went on to credit Boozer and Matuszak for their outstanding effort, and said he was pleased with the team's overall performance against a very good opponent. Winter added, "We play a lot of good teams this year. There are no 'puds' on the schedule."

The Wildcats won at the free throw line, hitting 42 out of 56 attempts. The Boilermakers actually scored eight points more from the field, but couldn't make up the point difference. K-State hit 39.1% from the field, scoring a record 45 points, 23 of them free throws. Matuszak made 19 points, Frank 16, and Long 10. Holwerda had six points and was a starter, but was replaced by Steve Douglas in the second half because (Tex said later) Holwerda was giving too much in height and not hitting as well as he could. Tex attributed that to, perhaps, Holwerda's change from a specialty player to a team player. Boozer led in rebounds with 16, while Matuszak had 11, Frank 10, Long five, and Douglas four.

Vs. INDIANA (12/6/58)
@HOME
WIN (Overtime) 82-79

As 12,000 fans watched in disbelief, K-State blew a 16-point lead, but rallied enough to trail by only five points with 2:41 remaining in the game. Foul trouble almost cost them the game as Boozer and Matuszak both went out with five fouls in the regulation time. Glen Long was sidelined with an injured knee. Winter went to the bench and found some heroes. Wally Frank put in two free throws to make it 69-70, but the Hoosiers countered with another streak, bringing them to a 76-71 edge and little time remaining.

Then Mickey Heinz hit a free throw, and Frank put in a jumper and a free throw to bring the Cats up to 75-76 with only 50 seconds remaining. Indiana's stall made the Cats foul several times, but the Hoosiers missed. Then, with ten seconds left, Price was fouled. He missed the first, but hit the second, tying the score.

In the overtime the Hoosiers made two free throws to go ahead, but Frank, Guthridge, and Heinz took over. Frank hit a field goal and a free throw before fouling out. Bill Guthridge hit two free throws with 1:19 on the clock. The scrambling efforts by Ballard, Holwerda, Heinz, and Price kept Indiana from scoring again and the Cats had the win against the powerful Hoosier team.

Indiana was playing with three sophomores: impressive Walt Bellamy who, at slightly over 6'10", gave Boozer a hard time, as did the other two sophomores, Herbie Lee and Bob Wilkinson. Bellamy and Lee fouled out in regulation time and Wilkinson was hit with his fifth foul during overtime.

Tex emphasized several key points. He had previously said that guard Don Matuszak was one of the most underrated players on the team and was just as important to the team as Bob Boozer, a point that became evident in this game. With Matuszak directing the attack, the Wildcats sailed along in good shape. They were up 21-11 when the fiery guard had to sit out with his third foul and the game was only seven minutes along. Before he got back, with two minutes in the half, Indiana had narrowed the gap to 42-35. Matuszak got his fourth foul just before intermission and sat out the first nine minutes of the second half. When he returned, Indiana was ahead 57-56.

Without Matuszak doing the playmaking, K-State had trouble sticking to its patterns. They proved vulnerable to a pressing defense. Following the victory, Tex commented that during the time-out and with only 2:50 on the clock and Indiana holding a five-point lead, Matuszak was suddenly doing all the talking. Tex said, "He wasn't urging them to win; he was telling them. I just stood back and let him have the floor. Even when he fouled out he still exerted his leadership through his talks at time-outs. We pulled out and won the game."

Winter was also correct in predicting that Indiana would be just as tough as Purdue. Their sophomores combined for a total of 46 points. Tex said that Walt Bellamy could become one of the game's super stars. He possessed the height, the agility, and could shoot a variety of shots. Against Boozer he played only 15 ½ minutes and scored 16 points. "He's a lot better than we thought he was," said Tex. "He's going to be a great one."

Tex also had plenty of praise for Glen Long and was optimistic that his injury would not keep him out long. Glen was becoming a key player and replacing him would be a hard job, as the combination of players seemed to be working very well.

Winter pointed out that Long was the kind of rebounder coaches love. "He not only is able to go up and get the ball away from men taller than is, but when he comes down he knows just what to do with it. Glen is one of our best passers, too," the coach said, "and he is the best man at getting the ball into the post." Filling his shoes would be the big job in workout next week. In the contention would probably be Steve Douglas, Mickey Heinz, and Cedric Price.

Vs. UNIVERSITY OF CALIFORNIA (12/12/58)
@ BERKELEY
WIN 68-65

The first half looked like it might be a Wildcat rout as the players seemed to hit from everywhere. The California Bears clogged the middle so most of the field goals were on outside shooting. By half-time K-State held a 45-36 lead. In the second half the Cats' shooting went cold and California warmed up. The Bears' Denny Fitzpatrick and Daryl Imhoff were their top scorers, with 13 and 12 points respectively.

The lead see-sawed in the last 6 ½ minutes and Cal took the lead at 57-56 with a free throw by Fitzpatrick, but a long set shot by Frank and a lay-up by Douglas on a feed from Matuszak on a fast break made it 60-57 for the Wildcats. Cal then went ahead 63-61, but Frank tied it at 63 with a long shot.

But K-State's Bob Boozer was not to be denied; he put on a superb performance despite the number of men dropping back to guard him. He scrambled for rebounding position when Frank got a shot up near the basket and tipped it in to put the Wildcats in the lead 66-65 with only ten seconds remaining. The Bears grabbed the ball and made two quick shots, but both failed. Matuszak took the rebound and was fouled. It was a one and one and he hit for both, making the final score 68-65.

Both teams took 65 shots from the field, with K-State hitting 29, and Cal hitting 28. Cal used a total of ten men in their line-up, while the Cats used only six. On the free throw line K-State had 10-14, while Cal went 9-16.

Boozer led all scorers with 27 points. Frank had 19, Ballard put in nine, Matuszak eight, Douglas four, and Holwerda one.

Vs. SAN FRANCICO (12/13/58)
@ SAN FRANCISCO
WIN 53-52

San Francisco came out fired up and determined to take the victory. The Wildcats were down by eight at the half and were hitting only 23% from the field. When they came back in the second half trailing 29-21, the Wildcats started playing inspired basketball. Matuszak hit for 11 points during the next 20 minutes, and Douglas provided four free throws in the final minute of play. The first two put the Cats on top 51-50 and when Douglas was fouled again only seconds later he calmly made another two to make it 53-50 with just eight seconds remaining. San Francisco made one last futile bucket at the buzzer.

Boozer again paced the Wildcats, scoring 21 points even though the S. F. Dons smothered him with defense. He hit two free throws to put the Wildcats ahead 49-46 with two minutes remaining and the Cats started a stall game. The Dons broke it and went ahead 50-49 with 1:08 on the clock and that set the stage for Douglas's free throws.

Douglas scored 12 points, Matuszak 11 and Frank three, with six points unaccounted for. Others in the game were Holwerda, Ballard, Graham, and Price.

Vs. BRIGHAM YOUNG UNIVERSITY (12/15/58)
@ PROVO
LOSS 77-68

It was obvious that the BYU team had a defensive strategy: to stop Boozer and collapse on him whenever he got the ball. Boozer wasn't in great shape going into the game, anyway, and BYU capitalized on that and held him to only eight points.

Wally Frank picked up the slack, and guard Matuszak hit for eight points from the outside in the first half. The Cats took the lead right away and built up a 27-23 advantage in the first half, but Gary Earnest, a 6' sophomore, attacked the Wildcat defense and scored 28 points, while forward John Nicoll added 21 as BYU stretched a slim 37-36 lead at halftime to a margin of 72-55 with four minutes left in the game.

Early in the second half Boozer was taken out with a sprained knee and wasn't able to get back into the game until only 8:30 remained on the clock and K-State was down 64-50. Cedric Price went in as a substitute and helped the Cats with a tip-in early in the second half, putting them ahead 40-39. But BYU refused to fold and, with Boozer out, took control of the game.

Tex Winter, in an almost desperate attempt, cleared the bench with 12:00 to go in the game and the Cats were trailing 53-45. BYU went even further ahead and the Cats were down 72-62 with 2:30 on the clock. Steve Douglas hit two free throws and two field goals in the final three minutes, but it wasn't enough. The Cougars were the victors by a large margin.

Wally Frank was K-State's high point man with his 18, Matuszak had 12, and Douglas finished with 11. Price contributed 10 as a reliever. Boozer had managed to put in only eight points, far below his average. Others scoring were Ballard with six, Holwerda two, Heinz one. Also playing were Guthridge, Graham, Balding, and Rice.

Vs. IOWA STATE (1/8/59)
@ AMES
WIN 59-56

The Wildcats came out strong during the first half of the conference opener and led 31-21 at intermission. In the next half they pulled away for a 13-point lead, 39-26, and seemed headed for an easy victory. However, the Cyclones started hitting from the outside over K-State's zone defense and came quickly to within four points, 37-41. Iowa State's center, John Krocheski, hit seven quick points, followed by a corner set shot by Ted Ecker, which gave Iowa State their only lead of the night. The lead returned to the Wildcats with a jump shot by Matuszak, making it 47-46. A foul shot by Ecker tied the game. Boozer then hit two jumpers, making the score 51-48. Two layups by Cedric Price and two free throws by Bill Guthridge finished the scoring and the Cats edged out another victory.

Iowa State played only six men, all of whom hit in double figures. For the Cats, Boozer had 18, Frank 14, Matuszak 10, Price seven, Ballard four, Johnson three, Guthridge two, and Douglas one.

Vs. COLORADO (1/10/59)
@ HOME
WIN 89-58

In this lop-sided victory, Bob Boozer played a nearly perfect game, hitting 11 of 18 from the field and nine straight from the free throw line, giving him 31 points before handing the game over to the reserves. The team shot at 49%, compared to Colorado's 28.6% K-State ran up a 12-4 lead as the game started and had built that to a 45-28 lead at halftime. They returned to the second half determined not to let that lead go, as Boozer and Frank led a sizzling rally that chalked up 14 points in the first 3 ½ minutes of the second half, compared to only five points for Colorado.

Coach Winter cleared the bench and even added the two football players, Cedric Price and Joe Vader, to the lineup. Colorado's Gerry Schroeder, who scored 28 points against K-State in the pre-season tournament, was held to just two field goals and one free throw and fouled out, with only five points.

Frank, Matuszak, and Price scored 10 points each, and eleven Wildcats were in the scoring column. Douglas had eight and Ballard seven. Others in the column were Guthridge with four, Holwerda, Graham, and Balding with two each, and Mickey Heinz with three. Douglas topped both teams with 12 rebounds.

Vs. OKLAHOMA (1/12/59)
@ HOME
WIN 90-45

Only two days after trouncing Colorado, K-State faced one of the biggest and strongest teams in the conference – Oklahoma University. But the Cats, who seemed to work as a team more and more in each game, were still on a rampage. They were now ranked #3 nationally.

Bob Boozer scored 27 points, 18 of those in the first half, and at intermission the Wildcats were ahead 38-21.

Opening the second half, Oklahoma's Denny Price was fouled by Ballard and made two free throws, but K-State countered by scoring 12 straight points to virtually put the game out of Oklahoma's reach. K-State hit 46.9 % on 30 of 64 attempts from the field, while the Sooners managed only 13 of 57 for 22.8%. From the free throw line K-state hit 30 of 42, while Oklahoma was 19 of 25.

When the Wildcats had a 35-point lead, 66-31, Tex cleared the bench. There was still 8:40 on the clock. Everyone saw action. Final scoring showed Frank and Ballard with 11 each; Holwerda with nine; Heinz and Douglas each added six; Price, Graham, and Guthridge each put in five; Matuszak had three; and Vader two. Also playing were Balding, Johnson, Rice, and Hamilton.

Vs. IOWA STATE (1/26/59)
@ HOME
WIN 78-55

Iowa State came prepared with a zone defense against K-State's ace shooter, Bob Boozer, and that did bother him some. He put in only 21 points – five below his average. As the Wildcats had often proved, though, when their All-American needed help he could count on it. The starting lineup supporters were Matuszak, Frank, Douglas, and Ballard. Three of those scored in double figures: Wally Frank scored 13, Steve Douglas 12, and Don Matuszak 11. Price had eight, Guthridge put in five, Holwerda and Graham two each, and Heinz shot for 2 from the field for four points.

Iowa State's center, John Krocheski, played hard against Boozer and also brought down 21 points, 17 of those in the first half. The big difference in the teams' playing, however, was evident on the boards: the Wildcats pulled down 55 to the Cyclones' 40; and at the free throw line the Cats made 22 of 27 while the Cyclones had only 13 for 18.

The game was fairly close during the first half, and with 5:30 to go, Cedric Price, Bob Graham, and Mickey Heinz all scored to open a 30-24 gap. Still, at halftime the Cats led by only one point, 30-29.

Shortly after the second half began, Frank and Matuszak downed free throws to start the surge. Then Douglas hit a hook and a lay in, and Boozer tipped one. The Cats were leading 46-37. Towards the end Matuszak played some of the best ball of the night. He hit one lay up, four free throws, and also fed Guthridge for easy goals twice on the fast break, once with a behind-the-back pass.

Essentially, Iowa State was out of gas and their coach began to put in reserves, as did Tex.

Vs. SOUTH DAKOTA STATE (1/31/59)
@ HOME
WIN 91-65

Showing lots of hospitality to veteran K-Stater Jim Iverson, who was coaching the South Dakota State team, the Wildcats used their reserves freely during the game and a total of 13 men took part for the Cats.

The Wildcats spurted to a 37-9 lead and limited the South Dakota Jackrabbits to just two free throws in the first six and a half minutes. In the second half, South Dakota State came back to trail by just 14, with the score at 57-43 before the Wildcats attacked again. Boozer, who would end up as top scorer with 24 points, hit seven quick points; and Cedric Price had a layup to make it 66-43. Wally Frank hit for 12; Steve Douglas, Don Matuszak and Jim Holwerda each had nine; and Price and Heinz each had 8. Others in the scoring column were Guthridge with five; Graham with four; Johnson one; and Sonny Ballard (playing his last game for the year) had two.

The game proved that the Wildcats could do just about everything well. The Jackrabbits were really never in the game except, ironically, in the rebounding. They trailed the Cats by only four rebounds, 65-61. Two of their players put in most of their points: Don Jacobsen with 23, and Marlin Van Den Einde with 22.

It was the 11th win in a row for the Wildcats.

Vs. NEBRASKA (2/27/59)
@ LINCOLN
WIN 50-43

During the first half of the game the lead changed hands several times and by half-time K-State held a narrow lead of 24-19. The Huskers came back again in the 2nd half ready to play, but Boozer and Heinz combined for five points, answering the Huskers' four, making the score 29-23.

Midway in the second half the Cats began to pull away. Wally Frank, who had had to sit out because of a fourth foul committed in the first half, came in at last and hit a set shot with 7:40 to go. That gave the Cats a lead of 40-30.

Boozer again led the scoring with 22 points on nine field goals and four free throws. Nebraska's Herschell Turner and Al Maxey had 16 and 14, respectively, but got little support from their teammates. Nebraska hit for only 28% compared to K-

State's 40% from the field. Others scoring for the Wildcats were Matuszak with nine, and Douglas, Heinz, and Frank with six each. Also playing were Guthridge and Price who had a free throw.

Vs. COLORADO (2/7/59)
@ BOULDER
WIN 70-59

With 1:33 left in the game, Colorado was behind by only four points, 55-59, and their high scorer, Russ Lind, was at the free throw line. He missed the shot and the Cats' Matuszak took charge. He darted with ease through a full-court press and first fed Wally Frank for a layup. Then he stole the ball, took a return pass from Douglas on a fast break, and stuffed it in. He was fouled on the play, however. The Buffalo's Schroeder protested the call and drew a technical. Matuszak missed his free throw, but Boozer scored on the technical for his 18th point. The lead was then 64-55.

Matuszak then made a crisp feed to Cedric Price for a layup, making the margin 11 points with only 53 seconds left. Price, a surprise starter, was the game's leading rebounder with 13. Frank had nine, Boozer seven, and Matuszak six. Colorado out-rebounded them 53-45. Matuszak had seven steals.

Boozer was the game's leading scorer with 18, followed by Frank and Price, both with 16. Matuszak scored 12, Douglas had seven, and Heinz one.

The Wildcats' record now stood at 17-1.

Vs. KANSAS (2/11/59)
@ HOME
Win 82-72

Although K-State was predicted to win this one, there was never any certainty when these state rivals played. KU had won the last six played in Manhattan. This game was played fairly evenly in the first half, ending at intermission with the score at 36-35 with the Wildcats ahead. The Cats were finally able to pull out a victory with an outstanding display of sheer determination.

The teams played catch up with each other during the first half, but KU dominated on the boards. K-State's excellent rebounder, Cedric Price, had three fouls and had to sit out much of the first half. As they went into intermission, Price had accumulated four fouls and other K-Staters were in foul trouble: Boozer, Frank, and Matuszak had three fouls each.

Bob Boozer was superb in scoring 33 points, even playing in foul trouble. He used a new fake and pumped in jump shots, layups, and hooks to counter the tremendous performance by KU's Bill Bridges, who had 28 points and 18 rebounds. The Jayhawks out-rebounded the Wildcats, 55-43.

The Wildcats fielded a new line-up: Boozer, Frank, Matuszak, Douglas, and now, Price. They used a man-to-man defense in the first half, then switched to a zone in the second half because of their foul problems. The second half belonged to K-State as Boozer caught fire. He made five field goals, and then Frank hit a long shot to put the score at 61-49 with 11 minutes left on the clock.

Boozer played the final 11:30 minutes with four fouls. Matuszak, also under fouling pressure, displayed his will to win with plenty of play making, plus his dribbling through a press, or faking and driving for a layup. He hit for 10 points. Frank hit for 13, Price and Douglas each had eight, Heinz added another six, and Holwerda put in four. Both teams scored well from the field. KU hit 25 of 59 for a 42.4%, while K-State made 33 of 71 attempts for a 46.5%.

Vs. OKLAHOMA STATE (2/14/59)
@ HOME
WIN 60-49

It was another great night for the Wildcats and for Boozer. He put in 27 points and edged his career total past the 1500 mark, to 1501 – to become the first K-Stater in history to go over that mark. Cedric Price led the games in rebounds with 11, and scored ten points. Don Matuszak and Wally Frank each got seven.

K-State hit 34.5% from the field in both halves. The Cowboys were on a shooting spree in the first half that kept the Cats under pressure. At intermission the Wildcats had the lead: 35-29. Coach Winter called for a zone defense in the second half, and that helped the Cats hold back the hot shooting of Oklahoma State's two big men, Arlen Clark, who finished with 20 points, and Dennis Walker, who scored 14.

The zone defense caused Oklahoma State to lose valuable time in their attack while K-State steadily increased the point spread. Finally, the Cats went back to a man-to-man and stopped the Cowboys.

K-state had a 52-40 lead with 9 minutes left when Cowboys Clark, Walker, and Bill Clarahan hit successive layups. Jim Holwerda, K-State guard, then made two free throws, cutting the lead to 54-46 with 6:08 on the clock. A minute later, the Wildcats started a scoring binge: Bill Guthridge hit a long jumper, and Boozer hit two jump shots to make the score 64-46 with 3:31 left. The Cats then put on a great defensive show that drew cheers from the 12,000 excited fans. Others scoring for the Cats were Holwerda with four, Douglas three, and Guthridge two.

Vs. OKLAHOMA (2/16/59)
@ NORMAN
WIN 75-55

The Oklahoma Sooners were never really in this game after they fell ten points behind midway through the first half. K-State's impressive big men added the exclamation point to the game with Boozer, still recovering from a charley horse, hitting for 21 points, while Wally Frank and Cedric Price added 16 each. Leading in rebounds was Matuszak with ten. He also canned nine points, shooting 4 for 7 from the field. Jim Holwerda added another seven for the Cats, while Douglas, Guthridge, and Heinz each made a field goal.

Oklahoma's guards, Raymond Lewis and Denny Price, kept them in the game with 20 and 18 points, respectively.

Tex called the game "well played as a team." He lauded the play of Boozer, Frank, and Price, and pointed out that each one had done a good defensive job too. He held particular praise for Wally Frank and called the Norman game Frank's best of the year. Tex also pointed out that Jim Holwerda had come back real well after being hurt and would help the team down the stretch.

Vs. OKLAHOMA STATE (2/21/59)
@ STILLWATER
WIN 62-50

The Oklahoma State coach, legendary Hank Iba, summed it up. "We did what we wanted to do for the most part. Oh, we made a lot of mistakes and did too much standing around when they sprung that zone, but I thought we played real well.

"This is a great team and I would like to see them go all the way. Boozer hurt us, but we figured he would. But, oh, that Matuszak, he's my ballplayer. And that number 51 – he did a great job as a reserve in the second half. That's a great team."

Number 51 belonged to Mickey Heinz and he continued to be impressive, for he got right into the ballgame as soon as he entered it. He scored four points and pulled in five rebounds in this game.

Tex Winter's team put on a defensive show on the Master of Defense's (Iba) own court. Tex used a man-to-man to start the game, and the Cats went into the lead, 14-13.

Tex then switched to a zone, and the Cowboys fell behind at the half, 30-26. The second half was a slow start for the Wildcats and their lead dwindled to 37-35 with 14 minutes left.

Then Boozer put on an All-American show. First came a tip, then a layup, then a free throw, and he followed with a jump shot for a 44-37 lead with 11:18 on the clock.

Matuszak provided excitement for the spectators with some of his great dribbling and added a five point shooting spree in the final 3 minutes to widen the margin. Cedric Price gave another fine performance, hitting 4 of 5 from the field and 3 for 3 from the line. K-State shot 47% from the field.

Both teams took a minimum number of shots, so rebounds were few. However, K-State had the edge with 31 to Oklahoma State's 26.

For the Cowboys, Arlen Clark and Bill Clarahan each had five rebounds, with Clark scoring 16 points and Clarahan and Soergel adding ten each.

Boozer led the Wildcats with 26 points. Price had 11, Frank nine, Matuszak seven, Douglas five, and Heinz four.

Vs. KANSAS (2/27/59)
@ LAWRENCE
WIN 87-77

Boozer, Price and Frank – K-State's towering trio – decided this game in the first 20 minutes. KU's Loneski was high scorer with 29 points, while K-State's Boozer had 28. Cedric Price threw in 16, all in the first half, while he kept his man, KU player Bill Bridges, to only four; and Wally Frank, who had some trouble covering Loneski, pumped in 17.

The game was not pretty, as any fan could testify. K-State had 20 errors and KU had 18 in the fast-paced game. But the hustle and determination of both teams was evident. Fouling was high. KU's Donaghue scored 15 but left the game on fouls with 15:50 left. Price was also out, at 10:30, and Bridges too, with 8:11 on the clock. K-State's Glen Long made his first appearance since an injury in the second game of the year and fouled out after only 6 minutes of playing time.

In rebounds KU came out on top, but only by one, 54-53. In shooting percentage, K-State was clearly the winner with 46% to KU's 31%.

In the first ten minutes the score see-sawed. When KU was leading at 20-19, K-State put in four baskets and was soon leading 33-23. KU pulled back to within four points, but the Wildcats answered with nine straight points, and it was 46-32 at halftime.

In the second half the Cats had a 16-point lead but Kansas player Dee Ketchum pumped in four field goals and the lead was narrowed to 71-65. K-State went into a delay game and sealed the win by hitting 11 for 12 from the free throw line.

Others scoring for the Cats were Matuszak with eight, Douglas with five, Holwerda and Guthridge each had four, Long three, and Heinz two. Commenting on the victory, Tex said he was happy that the team showed stronger rebounding than they had in recent games. He particularly cited Price's efforts on the boards.

The victory marked K-State's 18th straight win. They were now only two games away from a perfect Big Eight season. KU had scored a perfect conference record in 1946. The feat had not been accomplished since then.

Vs. MISSOURI (3/7/59)
@ HOME
WIN 108-69

The Cats matched their previous all-time high of 108 points, tying the record against Nebraska in 1953. Boozer saw more action than any of the other regulars as he played almost 27 minutes before drawing his fourth foul. Cedric Price probably played his best game so far and got in a lot of playing time before leaving. Boozer put in 32 points, while Price followed with 20. Matuszak, Frank, and Douglas sat out the entire second half after the Wildcats had built up a 59-37 advantage.

Kansas State played their entire bench, with 14 players getting in the action. Mickey Heinz had a field goal and a free throw. Glen Long made two baskets, Jim Holwerda had one basket and two free throws, Bill Guthridge tallied two field goals and two free throws, Bob Graham put in one field goal, Gary Balding had three baskets and 1 for 1 from the line, Joe Vader hit for a field goal, Jerry Johnson made three field goals and had 4 for 4 from the line, and Glen Hamilton played but didn't score. The three starters – Douglas, Matuszak, and Frank – had ten, seven, and one points respectively.

The Wildcats achieved their best accuracy of the season. They threw in 43 of 80 attempts for a 58.5%. The Tigers had a respectable 41% on 25 of 61. Boozer had 14 of 21 for 66% and

Price shot 9 of 14 for 64% as they led the Cats in a display of shooting every type of shot in the book.

Missouri was in the game during the first nine minutes and was trailing by only two with 11 minutes to go. Then K-State went into a zone and brought its lead up to 15 points before the Tigers scored again.

Tex felt badly about the score. He said they hadn't intended to break any records. He knew Sparky Stalcup, MU's coach, was in his worst season in 13 years and was being given a rough time by fans and alumni. Sparky, however, didn't feel that the Cats had tried to pour it on.: "I feel K-State is the #1 team in the country. They've got everything you want in a basketball team. This is the first time at Missouri I've had 100 points scored against me." Tex praised Cedric Price and called Boozer an All-American in more ways than just on the court. In fact, he had praise for the entire team.

Vs. NEBRASKA (3/9/59)
@ HOME
WIN 76-54

The final game…the seniors' big moment. And it turned out to be all they could have asked for. Seniors Boozer, Matuszak and Holwerda all enjoyed a memorable last home game. The crowd in Ahearn showed their appreciation with a lengthy standing ovation as the three were announced.

Nebraska formed a circle around K-State's big men and tried to keep the ball away from them. By the second half the Cats held only a slim seven-point lead. K-State had gone into a zone defense early in the game, but Nebraska kept coming back. Finally, in the second half, Tex took out Matuszak and put in Holwerda, known for his good set shot. Holwerda was on target this night and quickly pulled the Cats up to a wide margin by putting in four set shots. In the last ten minutes the Wildcats spurted out far ahead to take the big win.

Boozer tossed in 29 points for K-State, and Al Maxey and Herschel Turner were high for the Huskers with 16 points each. The Cats hit only 36.5% for the night, far off their last game's pace. The Huskers, though, hit only 32.4%. K-State won the rebounding, with 66 to Nebraska's 46.

Besides Boozer, other scorers were Price with 13, Matuszak with 11, Holwerda with ten, Johnson had five, Douglas put in four, Frank and Heinz each had two. Price led both teams in rebounding with 17. Boozer grabbed 11, Frank had eight, Johnson and Douglas had five, Heinz pulled down four, Holwerda three, Matuszak two, and Long one.

FORTY YEARS LATER

It was 1998, and the halftime of the Oklahoma State University vs. Kansas State University football game. The voice on the loudspeaker announced in a clear and decisive voice, "Please welcome back two of the winning-est basketball teams ever at Kansas State – the teams of 1958 and 1959." The stadium of approximately 40,000 people seemed to explode into a giant wave of humanity as the fans stood and burst into applause.

A photographer stood in the aisle taking pictures, and on the giant screen at the end of the field I could see the middle-aged men sitting beside me stand to acknowledge the applause. Glancing right and then left of me, I saw awkward smiles and embarrassed half-grins along with a few tears on the faces of these men who had been a part of each other's lives for 40 years. Some of them still saw each other on a regular basis, some only occasionally, and a few hadn't seen one another in years.

Forty years had passed since the first of the group had graduated, and now the players were back on campus for a reunion, the first in that long span of time.

Everyone had changed, of course, but we still knew each other. We recognized personalities, mannerisms, smiles, and heights. We had spent one evening and the next day getting re-acquainted, and found that we still shared the same camaraderie…same feeling of kinship. Tex and his wife, Nancy, were present, along with Pat

Shannon, who had lost Howie several years before the reunion. Ernie Barrett still worked at the university and was there for the reunion with his wife, Bonnie.

Here are brief summaries from the individual stories shared at the 1998 reunion:

Hayden Abbott went on to dental school, spent two years in the Air Force where he coached a national Libyan team. He eventually became an orthodontist and practiced for thirty years. A few years before the reunion, he had begun pursuing an interest in sculpting. He later presented a bronze bust of Coach Winter to the university.

Gary Balding left K-State with two degrees, in Electrical Engineering and Business Administration. He spent most of his working years in test equipment design for defense systems and in control logic design for large computer systems.

Sonny Ballard went into coaching for several years, then purchased his father's sporting goods store in Manhattan and expanded the business. He passed away a few years before the reunion.

Bob Boozer played in the Olympics in 1960 when the team won the gold medal. That team was inducted into the Olympic Hall of Fame. He participated in the NBA for 11 years, culminating with a world championship in Milwaukee in 1971. He spent 27 years with US West and ended his career as a federal lobbyist. In 1997 he was appointed to the Nebraska Board of Parole.

Roy DeWitz coached in the local high school for five years, then served as an assistant to Tex for two years. He became head coach at Augustana College for a year, then became an assistant coach at the University of Missouri. He went into the insurance business in 1970.

Steve Douglas became a professor of political science and Southeast Asian studies at the University of Illinois. He coached the national women's basketball team of Malaysia one year and was the first coach of the varsity women's basketball team at Illinois, serving in that capacity for two years.

Larry Fischer went into public accounting for about eight years. He then became associated with a medical company as a treasurer, eventually advancing to become Chairman of the Board.

Wally Frank played AAU basketball for four years, then worked in marketing for another eight years. He owned an oil distributing company for 19 years and is now an insurance agent/broker. He was named all Big Eight his senior year and was drafted second in the fourth round in the NBA.

Bob Graham played with Air Force teams after graduation and pursued his art degree by becoming an illustrator and graphic artist.

Bill Guthridge worked as a high school coach and teacher for two years, then became an assistant to Tex for five years before joining the basketball staff at North Carolina. He worked as an assistant coach for 30 years under Dean Smith, and, following Smith's retirement, took over the reins for three years.

Glenn Hamilton spent 32 years teaching and coaching and, at the same time, farming in his Kansas hometown. He passed away several years before the reunion.

Mickey Heinz was named the "Most Inspirational" player the next year. After graduation he attended OCS School and became the C.O. of Explosive Ordnance Disposal in the Navy. Serving numerous times in Vietnam, he also earned two masters degrees, in engineering and business. He died suddenly while playing basketball in 1979.

Jim Holwerda went into the field of education, as a teacher/professor/athletic director, and a coach at both the high school and college levels. He was named National H.S. Coach of the Year by USA Today.

Jerry Johnson spent 25 years as an Air Force and Reserve pilot and four years as Commander of the 190th Air Refueling group at Forbes. He owned a registered cattle business for 14 years, then a printing company. He's been very involved in racing and breeding thoroughbred horses.

Glen Long coached, then sold real estate for nine years before becoming involved in a pizza franchise. At one time this included 25 units and was his occupation for 31 years. He now manages some long-term leases on those properties.

Don Matuszak played AAU ball for two years, worked in the oil industry for four years, then returned to Manhattan as an assistant athletic director at K-State for several years. He joined a large corporation, ending up in management. After 25 years he opened his own management firm and ran leadership workshops across the nation.

Jack Parr spent a year in the NBA, then did college basketball officiating for ten years, also was a sporting goods wholesaler for eight years. He now has his own consulting/training business that is international in scope.

Dean Plagge spent two years in the Army, four years in business, then coached and taught in Kansas schools. For 26 years he served as a high school principal, then went into Human Resources with the school system.

Cedric Price lives in California where he owns a business franchise. In his senior year he was drafted 1st in the eighth round with the NBA.

Howie Rice worked in planning and economic development, then became a real estate agent and tax consultant.

Don Richards taught school and coached basketball and track for 14 years. Before retiring, he was a customer service representative for a construction company.

Joe Vader became a lawyer and established his own private practice, which he has run through all the ensuing years.

Two of the attendees, Chuck Hollinger and Bob Jedwabny, had ties to the 1957-58 team though they did not play that final year. Chuck played as a freshman, then transferred; Bob played for three years and sat out his senior year. Both men went into business: Chuck into sporting goods and Bob into insurance.

Howie Shannon, the assistant coach for the team, went on to become head coach at VMI and, after coaching, remained there on the staff. He passed away before the reunion.

Ernie Barrett, the other assistant to Tex, remained a loyal K-Stater and was always involved in his alma mater in some capacity. At one point he was the Athletic Director, then became the principal fund raiser. His loyalty and dedication have earned him the nickname "Mr. K-State."

Over the seasons Tex Winter steered the K-State teams to eight conference titles, and twice into second place. Four times his teams finished in the top ten nationally. In 1958 he was, as previously noted, named National Coach of the Year, and his 1959 team finished #1 in the season's final polls. In those two years alone, one of his players was named to the first team All-American, and three others were named to All-American honors.

After 15 years as head coach of the Wildcats, Tex Winter chose to step aside and move on because he thought he had become "stale" and the fans deserved someone new. Over the years he'd been offered coaching positions in many locations, some with great basketball traditions, some with troubled programs. In 1969 he headed to the University of Washington and accepted the challenge as head coach of the Washington Huskies. His motives were pure and simple. He felt that K-State could use some new blood, and he wanted to take Nancy, his wife, back to the west coast where she had her roots and where his three boys could enjoy an extended family. Tex felt that the style of play in the Pacific Coast conference, then dominated by John Wooden and UCLA, could help prove his theories on the game.

His secure position, an established program, and his legacy notwithstanding, Tex moved on, but would later claim Manhattan, Kansas, as his "home." To his credit, he never attempted to entice any of the players to go with him. His assistant, Cotton Fitzsimmons, who assumed the head coaching position, would say later that his time under Tex was one of his most enjoyable experiences.

For the next 14 years Tex moved around, even venturing into the NBA for several years. He continued using and perfecting his Triple Post Offense for which he's become famous in the world of basketball. Many coaches asked for his personal guidance and he was always willing to share his thoughts and techniques. One of those who came calling, Jerry Krause, became the general manager of the Chicago Bulls, and his first act, upon acceptance of his position, was to call Tex and ask him to join the staff. At the time, Tex and Nancy were considering retirement, but the lure of the game and the excitement of a new challenge stirred Tex to accept. It wasn't long before the Bulls were one of the top teams in the NBA. Tex eventually earned six NBA rings with the Bulls in his 13 years with the organization. When the team's coach, Phil Jackson, was later enticed to move to the L. A. Lakers, he asked Tex to join him. There, Tex helped bring the team three NBA championships.

Last Game for seniors.

AFTERWORD

Graduation, 1959. A joyful occasion that we had looked forward to for so long, yet how sad to say goodbye to our friends. Don and I had begun dating again only a month earlier. The magic between us was undeniable.

He had accepted a job offer from a well-known company. The offer included a career path and a chance to play AAU (Amateur Athletic Union) basketball, all for the great sum of $500/month. With that in his pocket, he proposed marriage.

My sights, though, were focused on a graduate assistantship in speech therapy at Iowa State (ironically, the place where Don and I had met). At the end of July I headed toward Ames, Iowa, but got only as far as Kansas City. My brother and his wife were living there and I spent the night. Our conversation that evening convinced me that I was making the wrong decision. A quick U-turn the next day sent me back home.

My name changed from Eaton to Matuszak three weeks later in a lovely church wedding. The next day we moved to Oklahoma, just in time for Don to meet his new work schedule.

As I noted earlier, almost forty years passed before Don's Wildcat team members and their wives went back to the campus for a reunion. Since then we have continued to meet every two or three years with the "old teammates." When we gather we still feel the old team spirit. Even the wives who did not attend K-State have told me they, too, sense that special bond.

The chemistry is still there.